PRAISE FOR BORDERLANDS

Written in thoughtful and beautiful prose, *Borderlands: Stories from an El Paso Shelter* captures the daily life of immigrant families and the experience of concerned volunteers striving for inclusion and justice for all living at the U.S./Mexico border. Deb Hansen connects struggles of families seeking an abundant life free from violence and impoverishment with the struggle for clean water and air, public health care, and the right to thrive not just barely survive. At a time when immigrants are being dehumanized and attacked, this book lifts up the dignity and humanity of all living in *la frontera*.

—Liz Theoharis, director, Kairos Center; co-chair, Poor People's Campaign

This memoir provides an emotional and thought-provoking view into the unique experience of offering hospitality at the border. Deb Hansen presents an artful vignette into the culture of care, compassion, and humanity fostered by everyone in this space, whether as volunteers or guests. She encapsulates the resilience and liminality of those at the border, amidst the ever-shifting landscape of geopolitics, policy enforcement, surveillance technology, and human need. She shows how communities of care can transform the violence of modern life. A must-read for understanding these profound human experiences.

—Shiva Darian, Assistant Professor of Computer Science, New Mexico State University

Deb Hansen takes us with her as she transcends the physical and emotional borders that stand between the suffering of people and planet and the creative transformation that she envisions and experiences as a volunteer at Annunciation House. Through the stories of those she accompanies—stories of displacement as a result of economic exploitation, climate change, war and racism, she weaves a tapestry of horror and hope, of pain and possibility, and most importantly, of a vision that calls us to compassion and collective healing.

—Kim Redigan, Meta Peace Team

In her very accessible account of her time at the U.S./Mexico border, Deb Hansen offers both memoir and analysis, along with stories of daily life, that make her experience come alive for readers. A self-confessed life-long "border crosser," Hansen weaves these stories of movement into a tapestry of difficult realities and inspiring hospitality in a simple, honest, and graceful way. She states that she will never be the same after these experiences, and neither will we as readers of this remarkable accounting.

—Mary Anne Perrone, Latin America Task Force, Interfaith Council for Peace & Justice

---

Borderlands touches our hearts in the way we need to be touched now. It introduces us to the *cotidiando*, the daily lives of our sisters and brothers, hidden behind the headlines. It offers community, hospitality, and care as an antidote to violence. *Borderlands* portrays life as an ecosystem, gently showing us how the violence against human bodies is the same violence inflicted on the land.

—Karina Breceda, *Fronteriza* maternal justice activist and artist at Stellar Shelter and Casa Maris

James Boggs often said, "We are nobody except in relationship to a whole lot of other bodies." Deb Hansen uplifts us all with this journey of accompaniment. She suggests that the path to becoming more fully human and living peaceably together is through caring, compassionate relationships. In these urgent times, relationships of mutual respect, responsibility, and reciprocity will transform our world and lead us closer to the beloved community.

—Richard Feldman, Boggs Center to Nurture Community Leadership

Deb Hansen's *Borderlands* gives readers a look into how U.S. politics' constant tinkering with asylum policies and rules causes needless but intentional emotional and physical suffering to families seeking asylum. The stories in here are as close as you will come to understanding the banality of evil as power-hungry individuals are willing to enact any policy for their dear leaders as they scapegoat innocents. The only humanity left in this moment comes from the victims and those tending to their needs with patience, grace, and humility.

—Jenn Budd, former Senior Patrol Agent in the U.S. Border Patrol, immigrant rights activist, and author of *Against the Wall*

BORDERLANDS

STORIES FROM AN EL PASO SHELTER

DEB HANSEN

APOCRYPHILE
PRESS

Apocryphile Press
PO Box 255
Hannacroix, NY 12087
www.apocryphilepress.com

Please join our mailing list at www.apocryphilepress.com/free. We'll keep you up-to-date on all our new releases, and we'll also send you a FREE BOOK. Visit us today!

CONTENTS

Today we have gathered and we see that the cycles of life continue.
We have been given the duty to live in balance and harmony
with each other and all living things.
So now, we bring our minds together as one
as we give greetings and thanks to each other as people.

Now our minds are one.

—"Words Spoken Before All Others,"
the Ohenten Kariwatekwen or Haudenosaunee
Thanksgiving Address

DEDICATION

To my ancestors who crossed the Atlantic from many places in the north and west of Europe to Turtle Island. They came for many of the same reasons people are leaving their homes, culture, language, and ancestral lands behind today: violence, poverty, loss of land, economic and climate instability, and persecution and extortion.

To the Indigenous peoples of the Americas and beyond who are reclaiming culture, land, and spirit, and are healing and shining in the aftermath of European colonization, broken treaties, and extreme violence. To the peoples trafficked to this land from Africa for their skills, talents, and labor, who have also been the targets of extreme violence, and are reclaiming power and respect through leadership, determination, and creativity.

To the emerging global healing movement and the courageous people who are facing, reckoning with, and grieving the pain of the collective historical traumas of the world that have displaced people in great numbers from their homelands.

To all those who are working to uphold our responsibilities to one another and to life, creating beauty and goodness in communities of care, honoring the stranger among us, and devoted to Earth as our precious home.

NOTE TO THE READER

The first names of volunteers and friends are their actual names. The first names of guests who have passed through our houses and given permission to share some of their experiences have been changed to protect their privacy.

This is your invitation to come on a journey to the borderlands. There are no promises of safety.

MAP OF THE SISTER CITIES[1]

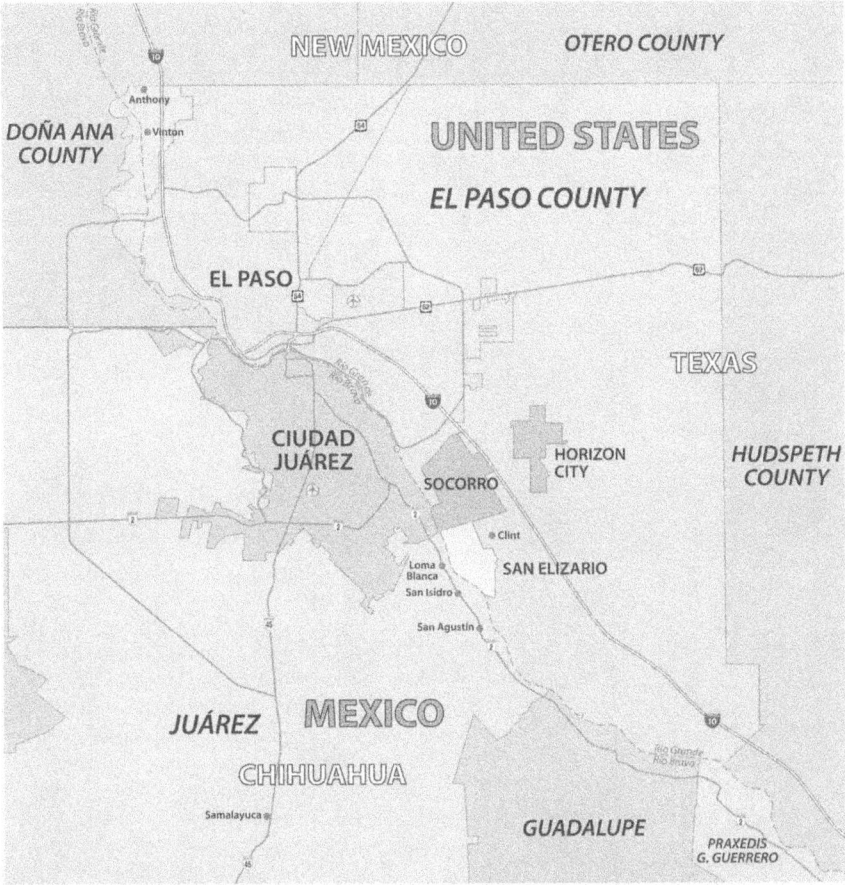

MAP OF BORDERS WHEN MOST OF THE
U.S. SOUTHWEST WAS PART OF MEXICO[1]

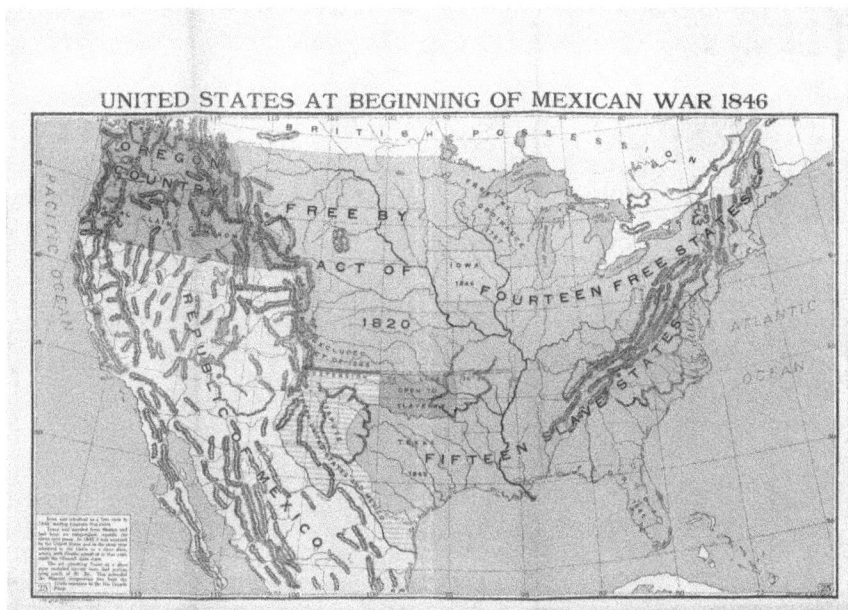

UNITED STATES AT BEGINNING OF MEXICAN WAR 1846

MAP OF EARLY INDIAN TRIBES[1]

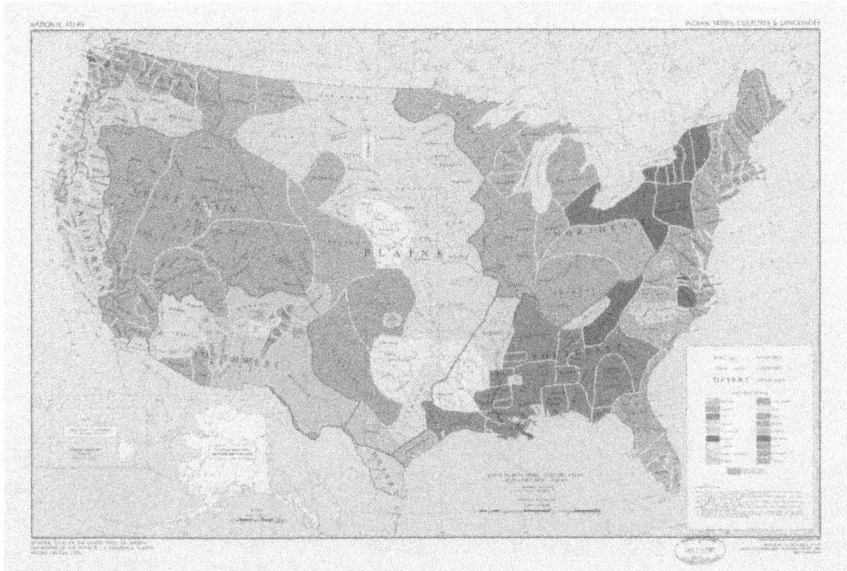

A PILGRIMAGE TO THE BORDERLANDS

ANSWERING THE CALL

My train is held up on the tracks just blocks away from the El Paso train station, my final destination. Nearly an hour goes by with no explanation. As we finally pull into the station, someone tells me that seven people on the train were taken into custody. There were no other details. Welcome to a new reality at the borderlands between the United States and Mexico. It is a world I have no experience with.

It is November 2019. I've been on a train for three days from Michigan to Texas, and I'm eager to complete the long journey. For the next five months, I will be living and working in a shelter for people seeking asylum in the United States. My Spanish is limited. I've never done this type of work, but I'd been feeling a call to go to the border for nearly a year. It wouldn't go away.

It's not the first time I've received a message like that which made no sense. I've learned to trust these niggles. The clarity for them often appears only in hindsight. So here I am on another unexpected turn on the labyrinth of my life, a meandering and ultimately purposeful path.

But why was I being called to the borderlands? I wasn't totally sure at the beginning. More clarity on this would come over my three winters in El Paso, Texas. At home in Michigan, in addition to my work with people, I've advocated for access to affordable water, protecting the Great Lakes, and energy democracy in a time of rapid climate destabilization. What I was clear on is that I wanted to see for myself what goes on in the borderlands. I also knew that my intention was to treat the people I would encounter with the same respect and dignity that I would want for myself in similar circumstances.

Besides, I've been a border-crosser for all my adult life. It began with a keen interest in languages and cultures. In college, I spent half a year living and studying in a remote part of France. There I became fascinated by the variety of ways people of different ethnicities and cultures see the world. This theme continued with diverse friendships, Interfaith studies and ordination, community service, and hospital and hospice chaplaincy.

How did I end up in El Paso? I had asked Zeb, a friend from my seminary days in Berkeley, California, for the names of a few organizations to explore. Zeb had clearly found his path somewhere at the border. I couldn't remember where he was living, but was confident he could help. "You go to Annunciation House," was Zeb's brief reply. I looked at the website and found it compelling. It was a relief not to have to look further.

Annunciation House is an independent, privately-funded network of shelters and congregations for people seeking asylum in the U.S. The core network is in El Paso and New Mexico, and stretches from there, as needed, into Dallas, Missouri, Nebraska, New Hampshire, and more. The organization has been providing this hospitality for decades. Founded in 1978, it began with a group of young Catholics who wanted to live with greater purpose through solidarity with and service to the poor. After months of living in the *segundo barrio* or second ward, they saw that the people most in need were undocumented, and for that reason, turned away by other social service agencies. Soon after, El Paso began to see large numbers of people from Central America who were fleeing unstable or violent situations in their home countries.

These houses hold a lot of history. They are places of hospitality and grace, offering sanctuary and practical support for people from outside the United States who are seeking refuge from violence, poverty, climate destabilization, and more. They serve as a waystation, an oasis in the storms of life.

Places like this are also prayers of possibility. They offer a lived experience of mutual respect, relationship, and solidarity. Annunciation House adapts to ever-changing conditions and policies thanks to a supportive and generous community that extends well beyond the shelters.

Just as people in migration enter liminal space when they leave their home country behind, my three journeys to El Paso have also been a pilgrimage—a journey of discovery. The sections of this book reflect the three stages of a pilgrimage: initiation, a time of orientation where everything is new and unfamiliar; purification, a time of intensity and testing where the old life is gradually stripped away; and rebirth or transformation, an unanticipated shift in perspective. After these experiences, my life will not be the same again.

INITIATION
NOVEMBER 2019 – MARCH 2020

*We split the world into pieces and called them countries. We claimed
ownership over something that never belonged to us. We created barriers
where barriers should have never been, but migration has always been
something that comes naturally to humans [and other living beings like
birds and caribou] regardless...*
—Carla Soto Guerrero

Bea, a Catholic sister and one of the volunteers I'll be working with,
is there to meet me at the train station, as promised. She had called
to introduce herself while I was en route. I liked her immediately. She
is an elder originally from Ireland, full of life, sharp as a tack, dedicated to the people we serve, and lots of fun.

I've been assigned to Casa Vides, the smallest of Annunciation
House's three shelters that offer hospitality not just to people from
Latin America, but well beyond. A fourth shelter, the organization's
original home, is closed for major renovations.

I'm more than a little apprehensive about my work schedule. I'd
mentioned my declining energy level in my application. In fact, I

mentioned it several times. I had spoken with someone who had volunteered for two weeks at the shelter called *Casa de los Refugiados* (CDR) or House of the Refugees. It's the organization's high-volume shelter. At its peak, this shelter could handle the arrival of 500 to 600 people a day. It sounded like one big hive of activity, and I wasn't sure I could sustain that pace.

Volunteers are expected to work six days a week. Once a month, I will get two days off in a row. Assuming I survive my first three months, I'll get a week off. That week is already planned. I will join a study group in Cuernavaca, Mexico for ten days. A friend who has organized similar expeditions in the past invited me to come along. It sounds like the perfect complement to my initiation to the Spanish-speaking world and our neighbor to the south.

During my first few weeks at Casa Vides, the team included four volunteers, including me. One will leave in a few months and a fourth and fifth person will join us later.

My Spanish proves to be adequate to respond to or make simple requests:

"May I have a toothbrush?"

"Do you need toothpaste too?"

"The baby is out of diapers."

"What size do you need?"

Answering the phone and attempting a conversation in Spanish makes my stomach clutch. I want to be able to have meaningful conversations with our guests. I am interested in getting to know them and hearing their stories and concerns. That's not possible this time, but I pick up languages fairly easily and still speak fluent French.

Covid-19 hasn't come to the U.S. yet, but we know it's only a matter of time.

This first journey to El Paso is an initiation into relationship with people whose lived experience is so different from my own in ways that are nearly impossible to imagine. Their resilience leaves me unsettled and in awe. I am convinced I would be broken by the physical, emotional, mental, and spiritual trials of the journey north from Latin America and other places.

Every day, I experience new challenges in the work. It is demanding in every way. The rewards are beyond measure.

NOVEMBER 2019

NOVEMBER 10, 2019

Before leaving Michigan, I hear there are 15,000 people in detention in Tijuana, Mexico. Detention is the government's practice of holding people in custody while they wait to learn if they will be deported or allowed to remain in the U.S. until their day in court. People who've been in detention, often for months, call it jail. I'm not sure what to expect in El Paso with the new Migrant Protection Protocols.

According to the U.S. Department of Homeland Security (DHS) website, "The Migrant Protection Protocols (MPP) are a U.S. Government action whereby certain foreign individuals entering or seeking admission to the U.S. from Mexico—illegally or without proper documentation—may be returned to Mexico and wait outside of the U.S. for the duration of their immigration proceedings, where Mexico will provide them with all appropriate humanitarian protections for the duration of their stay... The U.S. is facing a security and humanitarian crisis on the Southern border."[1]

I'm told the numbers of people coming through our shelters have dropped significantly as a result of MPP in the past few months. Border cities in Mexico tend to be quite dangerous and have little to do with "protection."

Applicants for refugee status or asylum—a legal protection that allows people from other countries to remain in the U.S.—must establish that they fear serious harm in their home country on the basis of race, religion, nationality, membership in a social group, or political views.

Laws have not kept up with the realities of these times. As global climate destabilization continues to unfold, we can expect the numbers of displaced people to swell exponentially. It is a moral dilemma with no easy answers. If the local economy is devastated by war or trade deals—or you live on an island or coastline that is threatened with sea level rise—or the rains don't come, and the scorching heat no longer allows food to be grown where you live—none of these things are a legal reason to flee your home and seek refuge elsewhere.

The train from Dearborn to Chicago looks like the Polar Express.

BECAUSE I WORK on energy and climate, I am taking the train. Train travel emits significantly less carbon into the atmosphere than air travel. Besides, it's a great way to relax, meet people, and see the countryside. At the start of my journey south, the train from Dearborn to Chicago looks like the Polar Express, with ten inches of new snow.

NOVEMBER 17, 2019

I already feel at home at Casa Vides. There were three families, including a two-week-old baby, living here when I arrived. Now there are two. Both families are long-term guests who need a sponsor who can take financial responsibility for them until their asylum cases are decided by an immigration judge. Our guests sleep on bunk beds in dorms or in smaller rooms. We ask them to prepare the meals and help keep the house clean and in good order. Volunteers make sure the pantry, clothes closet, and clinic are stocked, handle the house laundry, answer the door and the phones. We eat together and share the cleanup and other chores.

CASA VIDES IS NAMED in memory of Gabriel and Gladys Estela Vides from El Salvador. Gabriel sent their eldest son to the U.S. after his mother was assassinated for her work in labor organizing and her participation in union strikes. The son had been kidnapped and tortured by the government's intelligence operation. Vides wanted people in the U.S. to understand what was going on in his country. Eventually, he was also killed. Annunciation House's director, Ruben Garcia, became the guardian for the six Vides children.

This stunning mural in the dining area is a tribute to those who died during the years of extreme violence in Central America. In the early years of Annunciation House, many people from the Northern Triangle of El Salvador, Guatemala, and Honduras had fled bloody civil wars and were given shelter and support. It is still not generally understood in this country that the U.S. was heavily involved in these wars, providing funding, military advisors, and training.

Patricia Malcolm, the New Mexico-based artist who painted the mural, lived in this shelter for several months to get a sense of our guests. She also traveled around Mexico and Central America to better understand the situation in their home countries. Pat and her husband had been involved in the sanctuary movement of the 1980s and fostered many teens and young adults. In addition to this mural, she painted murals in El Salvador in the 1990s to encourage communities as they rebuilt.

The stunning mural at Casa Vides by Patricia Malcolm.

All of the people in the mural, except the Vides couple, were guests here during her stay. The mural includes the prophetic quote of Oscar Romero: "If they kill me, I will rise again in my village." Archbishop Romero, an outspoken critic of the war and proponent of respect and liberation for the poor, was assassinated while saying Mass in San Salvador. If you look closely at the mural, you will find faces and body parts in memory of those unknown who were killed by death squads.

The names of those who were killed in El Salvador, painted like vines or waves around the pillars of the great room, are only hundreds of the thousands collected by the Central American

Resource Center at the University of Texas at Austin. Those conscripted into the death squads faced threats on their lives if they refused to do this ugly work on their own people. Annunciation House has provided housing to several death squad members who fled the terror of the times in Central America. It is my first time being exposed to these harsh realities and the direct involvement of this nation.

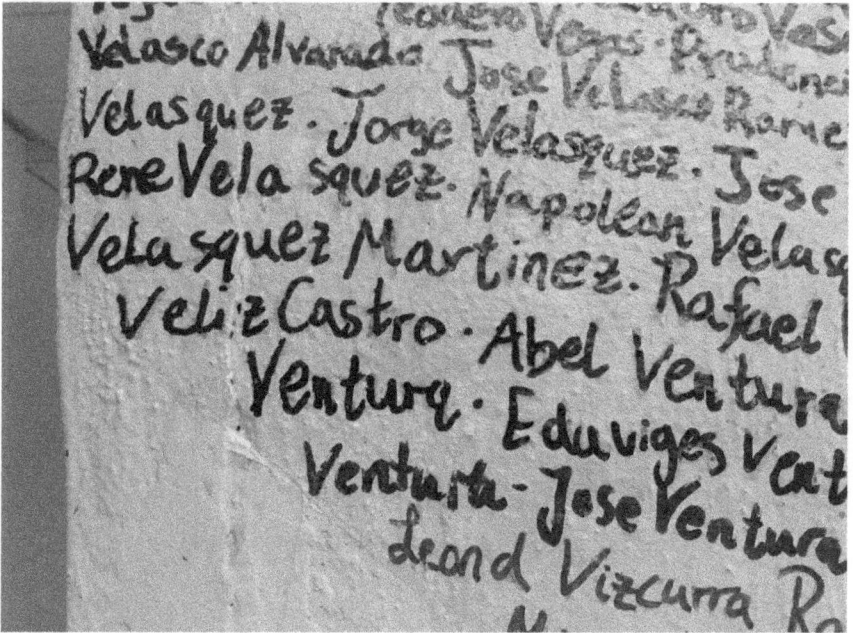

The names of those who were killed in the U.S.-backed dirty war in El Salvador wrap around the pillars of the great room.

At the bottom of a set of very steep stairs is a clothes closet and a clinic where over-the-counter medications are kept behind a locked door. There's also a pantry, a craft room, storage for seasonal items, and a shop stocked with basic tools to make simple repairs. At the far end of the basement, there is a comfy space where the groups of visitors we host can sit in circle and reflect on their experiences at the end of each day.

There are also reminders of difficult realities... The names of those who died in the desert are recorded on painted ribbons that wrap around the columns like the ones upstairs. These people were mothers, fathers, sons, and daughters, like you and me.

It's been almost twenty years since the nineteen-year-old young man in the downstairs mural, Juan Patricio Peraza Quijada, was living at Annunciation House, the first of the organization's shelters. He was about to journey to San Francisco to start a new life.

Mural of Juan Patricio Peraza Quijada, a 19-year-old guest at Annunciation House, was shot and killed by a U.S. Border Patrol agent.

One morning, after taking out the trash, he went back outside to talk with friends. An unmarked car with two uniformed patrol agents pulled into the parking lot. The agents confronted Juan Patricio. When a volunteer came out of the shelter to see what was going on, the young man ran. A chase ensued. One of the agents caught him and hit him on the head with a baton. Juan Patricio continued to run, found a steel pipe, and brandished it above his head. The agent did not shoot and called for backup. After the additional support arrived, agents formed a semi-circle around Juan Patricio on San Antonio Avenue with their guns drawn. The last agent to arrive on the scene shot and killed him forty-five seconds later. A grand jury declined to indict the agent, and although Juan Patricio's parents later brought a civil suit against Border Patrol, it was found not to be at fault. It is a familiar story.

This year Juan Patricio's name was read for the first time at the solemn funeral procession at the School of the Americas Watch vigil, the grassroots movement to close the infamous School of the Americas (SOA), a U.S. military training institute for Latin America. "Juan Patricio Perada Quijada. *Presente!*" Your spirit is here among us.

———

IN ADDITION TO OUR GUESTS, there are groups of university students or members of congregations that come to El Paso regularly for a program called Border Awareness Experience (BAE). These groups are usually here for a week and spend their days out and about in the community. They might visit a shelter and prepare the evening meal, listen to a presentation by a Border Patrol agent, learn about the history of the sister cities, spend a day in Juárez, and sit quietly in a park, gazing at the signs of extreme poverty just across the border in Anapra, Mexico. Participants often say that what they see from the park is the most powerful experience. Do borders function to preserve inequities?

Casa Vides offers hospitality to these BAE groups. I enjoy getting to know them and hearing about what impressed them. The last group scheduled for 2019 returned home yesterday. They left inspired and committed to explore the possibility of starting their own initiative to help resettle people from other lands in their community. The house is quite quiet today.

Our volunteer team at Casa Vides: (from left) Chris, the author, Rosaleen, and Bea.

THIS IS our volunteer team at Casa Vides. Bea (right) is our house coordinator. She had a career as a teacher and principal in Texas. She also worked in Mexico for many years. She runs a tight ship, is a multitasker extraordinaire, and is always thinking ahead about the next challenge. She makes steel-cut oatmeal for us along with soups and avocado salad. I'm learning so much from her. Bea takes new volunteers under her wing. She makes sure I'm introduced to people in the larger community.

Rosaleen sits behind her. Also originally from Ireland, she is another Catholic sister. Rosaleen lived and served in Peru for thirty-eight years. She was a nurse and attends to the basic health needs of our guests.

Chris is in his second year doing this work at the border. He is a sensitive individual who carries many responsibilities. He plays guitar and is also a songwriter. He will be with us for a few more months.

Caroline, another sister originally from Ireland, will join us later. She is jolly and hard-working. She has worked here before and will make sure the pantry is stocked with staples. She's always up early and makes sure cereals and bread are available for breakfast and the coffee pot is on.

Carol has worked in the Peace Corps and on behalf of the Mary-knolls who have a reputation for their service in very difficult conditions. She worked with her family among the poor in Bolivia, including on a floating clinic, and later in Western Samoa. She will join us near the end of my stay.

NOVEMBER 18, 2019

Many of our guests come from Central America. So far, I haven't seen anyone from Costa Rica or Panama. *Central American Migration: Root Causes and U.S. Policy*, a 2019 report from the Congressional Research Service (CRS) states, "An estimated 250,000-300,000 people have left the turbulent Northern Triangle...in each of the past five years, with the majority bound for the United States."[2]

I want to understand how the violence and economic conditions that cause so many of our guests to flee their homes and ancestral lands are directly connected with the actions of the U.S. government. Here's an example:

The Department of Defense runs a training institute for Latin American military and police forces. The School of the Americas, was founded in 1946 and operates at Fort Benning, Georgia. Its graduates come from countries with repressive, authoritarian regimes known for violence against their people.

The flag flying over the barbed wire at Fort Benning (now called Fort Moore), Georgia, home of the School of the Americas.

The school has been connected with U.S.-backed dirty wars, a brutal form of state terrorism in Central and South America. In addition, graduates of the SOA, nicknamed the School of the Assassins, have fomented coups and disappeared, tortured, and murdered political opponents around the world. Because of its increasingly problematic reputation, the SOA was rebranded in 2001 as a security alliance, the Western Hemisphere Institute for Security Operation (WHINSEC). Fort Benning would later be renamed Fort Moore.

In 1996, the Pentagon made SOA training manuals available to the public. They included sections on torture, extortion, and execution. People who pass through our shelters have lost colleagues, family members, and friends as a result. There has never been an independent investigation into the SOA.

The participants are solemn as the the names and ages of the murdered by those trained at the school are read aloud.

This year's annual SOA Watch vigil ended yesterday at the gates of Fort Benning. The SOA Watch was founded in 1990 after the massacre at the University of Central America in El Salvador carried out by SOA graduates.

I participated in these vigils in 2013 and 2014. They are incredibly moving. They include education, music, vendors, and an evocative ritual on the last day. At that ritual, the names and ages of the murdered are solemnly read, one by one, as everyone processes around the gates of the base. Many are moved to tears. Many knew the victims personally. Since the great majority of people from Latin America are Catholic (and now increasingly Evangelical Christian), everyone in the procession raises a cross with one or more of these names and intones "*Presente!*" Your spirit is here among us. The crosses are then placed in the cyclone fence.

The vigil to shut down the School of the Americas.

TODAY THE VOLUNTEERS from all three houses are getting together for a reflection, brunch, and business discussion. Some volunteers have been here for years. The rest of us are either young people who've committed to a year or like me, are here for several months. I like the diversity of age, background, and life experience.

The values and spirit of Annunciation House are based on Catholic social teaching. In my own Interfaith study and service, I find these teachings comparable to Tikkun Olam, the healing and repair of the world, from the Jewish tradition, the engaged Buddhism modeled by Thich Nhat Hanh, the duties of the human family described in the Haudenosaunee Thanksgiving Address, and others. Volunteers of all ages come from a variety of wisdom traditions or claim none. Most of us are European American.

There is so much to learn. Back at the house, I get a call from someone in tears who has had undocumented people living with her. She wonders if we can help.

Someone living in another state will spend the night with us. She has an Immigration and Customs Enforcement (ICE) check-in tomorrow morning.

We hear that some unaccompanied young people who had crossed the river have decided to turn themselves in after consulting with an attorney.

NOVEMBER 19, 2019

Rosaleen often takes a stroll by herself after dark. She invited me to join her the evening I arrived. I was surprised an elder would go out on her own at night. I had no idea that for the past twenty years El Paso has consistently ranked among the safest cities in the nation for similar sized cities. Just across the border in Ciudad Juárez, it's another matter. It's sad to hear people talk about how much they enjoyed visiting Juárez before it became so violent, and the borders became so hardened and militarized.

Beautiful holiday lights adorn San Jacinto Plaza for WinterFest.

Casa Vides is located downtown near the oldest part of the city. We walk past the minor league baseball stadium to San Jacinto Plaza, the main square where the trees are adorned with festive lights for WinterFest. Live alligators used to inhabit a large pond at the center of the square.

NOVEMBER 21, 2019

When I visit the El Paso History Museum, I'm not sure what to make of this exhibit with flashing lights, riffing playfully on an old-fashioned ice truck with quite another purpose. It is positioned prominently near the entrance.

ICE truck or ice truck? A strange exhibit at the El Paso History Museum.

NOVEMBER 22, 2019

It's taken a village to get the kids who will be staying with us for a while enrolled in school. The El Paso school system is understanding, welcoming, and bilingual. Two of the little ones are still achy from yesterday's vaccinations. We get them registered online today—a laborious and mind-numbing process that requires both a volunteer and a parent.

One of the volunteers is down with the flu and quarantined upstairs for a week. Most of the rest of us have colds. I am looking forward to a day off on Sunday. Our director will be cooking Thanksgiving dinner for the volunteers from all three houses. I'll be making cranberry sauce tomorrow during my shift.

Thanksgiving is not celebrated in Latin America. Schools in Mexico closed all week for Day of the Dead festivities earlier in the month.

NOVEMBER 23, 2019

In the kitchen, there is often more going on than good cooking. Sometimes there are tears, stories of betrayals, violence, fear, facing the unknown, and coming to grips with all that has been left behind. When my Spanish fails, I sense the feelings. There is also laughter, the sweetness of the children, community, and the peace of a sanctuary.

"We will protect each other," reads the subtitle of a poster on one of the refrigerators.

There is often more going on in the kitchen than good cooking.

NOVEMBER 23, 2019

My shift begins at 7 a.m. I put out breakfast and make coffee. The volunteer staff meets for a check-in and reflection after we eat. I spend the rest of the morning with the children, making Thanksgiving decorations.

There's a dinner of homemade potato flautas, soup, and ice cream to celebrate a birthday.

Just when I'm ready to wrap things up and relax, our director drops off two young adults. It takes time to register new guests. I ask for immigration papers and contacts, make phone calls to sponsors, offer food and a set of dry, clean clothing. I show them to the showers and assign them a bed. These are the first new arrivals since I arrived.

It's also my first look at immigration papers. These papers mean guests are in the system and in the beginning of the deportation process. They've been assigned an alien or A-number—a term that denies our common humanity—and a court date, sometimes more than a year out. They'll have an opportunity to make a case for asylum. Almost everyone has a sponsor, typically a family member who is already here. Volunteers call each new guest's sponsor with details they need to know to make travel arrangements by bus, train, or plane. These papers give our guests permission to travel to their sponsor anywhere in the country. If shelters like these didn't exist, people would be dropped off at a bus station, the airport, or on the street.

Rosaleen and I decide to take a short walk to get some fresh air. When we get back, it's around 11:30 p.m. I'm calling it a day.

NOVEMBER 24, 2019

People from the community are always stopping by with something to offer the house. This morning, someone drops off six loaves of a festive, home-baked holiday bread. I decorate the tables before the other volunteers arrived for our early Thanksgiving dinner and postpone my day off until tomorrow.

A Thanksgiving celebration for the volunteers.

NOVEMBER 25, 2019

A word about the organization's other shelters...

The original shelter, known as "A-house," is closed for major renovations during my entire stay.

Casa de los Refugiados is a converted warehouse that can accommodate up to 500 people. Guests sleep on Red Cross cots. All meals are brought in by organizations like the Salvation Army. There are porta potties in lieu of bathrooms. Volunteers in this shelter are in perpetual motion. The guests are there for just a night or two.

Another shelter, Casa Oscar Romero, can accommodate around 100 people and is located near the El Paso Detention Center. Romero also offers hospitality to Mexican widows (and on a rare occasion, widowers) who are entitled to their deceased spouse's Social Security benefits. These people used to stay at Casa Vides and some continue to knock at our door, unaware of the change.

To receive these benefits, they are required to present themselves at a Social Security office in the U.S. every month to sign for the check they will receive later in Mexico. Or if that is too inconvenient, they have the option to come twice a year and stay for an entire month each time. What is this about? I wonder if eligible people living in other countries have the same requirement. It seems punitive.

The house I've been assigned to, Casa Vides, offers shelter primarily for long-term guests who could be with us for months. I have heard stories about families who lived at Annunciation House for years. It is not a high-volume operation like the other houses. Most of the BAE groups who stay with us come on spring break or semester break. We can accommodate around fifty people. It feels more like a home.

Most of the people who pass through our shelters have been released by Border Patrol and ICE. Our director maintains relationships of trust with these authorities. That means we know in advance how many people will be dropped off at each of our shelters every day, the approximate arrival time, and any circumstances we need to be aware of. These people come to us in buses and vans. Some are transported from locations in New Mexico. Sometimes new arrivals do not know what city or state they are in.

NOVEMBER 26, 2019

It seems like a good idea to get some exercise on my day off by walking over the Paso del Norte bridge, only a ten-minute walk from the house. I plan to stay on the bridge and not enter Mexico. I don't realize that the border is actually at the top of the bridge immediately over the Rio Grande. I no sooner pay my fifty cents and pass security when I realize I have no ID on me. Oops.

On the Paso del Norte bridge spanning the Rio Grande that defines the U.S./Mexico border.

The guards won't let me go back, but tell me I can walk across the traffic to the other side. I cross as they suggest, waiting in a long line, breathing exhaust from the cars. After entering the large building, I explain my mistake to the agent at the counter. He asks for my name and date of birth, looks me up on the computer, and I'm good to go—even on time for dinner.

It's not the first time something like this has happened. Something in me doesn't relate to political borders. I remember my parents announcing that we were about to cross the state line on a car trip. I must have been around eight years old. There wasn't any line. I looked!

More times than I care to mention, I've arrived at an airport for an international business flight and was sent home to get my passport. In Michigan, we used to be able to drive back and forth to Canada with an ordinary driver's license.

Political borders are made up by the powerful. They aren't real in the sense that a forest, a mountain range, or a river is real.

NOVEMBER 28, 2019

It's Thanksgiving Day. Volunteers from the community cover for us on days like this. Our families also get to enjoy an outing together at the San Jacinto Plaza. Border Patrol and ICE aren't releasing anyone today. This makes it easy for us. For those detained, it's another day in "jail."

We are treated to an in-home ukulele concert performed by an ensemble from Singapore, France, and Kansas before and after a traditional meal at the home of some friends of the house. Delightful!

Afterwards, Chris drives us up the mountain to Scenic Drive so we can enjoy the view over the city and the Sierra de Juárez mountains at dusk. Then we cruise through the campus of the University of Texas at El Paso (UTEP) where the architecture evokes Bhutan and fits in beautifully with the landscape.

NOVEMBER 29, 2019

An elder and her adult son appear at our door today after walking across the bridge from Juárez. The woman's feet are sore. She is here to fulfill the requirement to receive her Social Security death benefit from her deceased husband. She was ill last month and missed her monthly visit, so now she must spend an entire month in the U.S.

She was given our address for hospitality and didn't register online. After making a call to Casa Oscar Romero to make sure there is room for her, we offer them bus fare. It is too far to walk.

NOVEMBER 30, 2019

A few of us go to see a documentary called *The River and the Wall* in the afternoon. The theme is the continuous border wall being built along the 2,000-mile U.S./Mexico border. The beauty of the scenery is breathtaking. Missing from the film are local Indigenous voices and a historic context.

Walls come and go. Was it the same impulse that led to the construction of Hadrian's Wall, the Great Wall of China, the Berlin Wall, and Detroit's Eight Mile Wall?

DECEMBER 2019

I enjoy a game of hide-and-go-seek with a five-year-old who is new to the house. Later, I take a break and explore the *Duranguito* just a few blocks away. It's one of the oldest *barrios* or neighborhoods in El Paso. But it is slated to be demolished so a new arena can be built. The struggle to preserve it was later successful.

Duranguito, one of the oldest barrios or neighborhoods in El Paso, is just a few blocks away from Casa Vides.

DECEMBER 2, 2019

We now have eight young people in the house ranging in age from three weeks to fourteen years. Parents are responsible for supervising their children, but they need a break too. We have books, games, puzzles, and movies available to keep them entertained. The younger ones love to be read to. But even fairy tales are tough going when you're just learning Spanish.

A community volunteer picks up a mom and kids at 7:15 a.m. for a follow-up doctor's visit after a child's discharge from the hospital.

Chris makes two trips to the elementary school in the morning. The parents of two of the kids meet with a counselor in the afternoon. By the end of the day all five of the new children are enrolled in school. Our three-year-old is a candidate for a preschool program for children from low-income families. We all feel it will do him and his mother good, but that's work for another day.

We get word that a total of 160 people are going to be released from custody in our geography. The volumes are going back up since MPP, nicknamed "Remain in Mexico," was implemented in August. We are told that our house will receive sixteen of them, all from Brazil. No one here speaks Portuguese. In cases like these, Google Translate is our friend!

Activity is an antidote to boredom for our guests. Some of them help clean the ceiling fans and wash windows and curtains. A representative of the Catholic diocese arrives to explain the trauma-informed therapy they can offer to two of our guests.

Two people from Chihuahua arrive, looking for lodging while they fulfill their Social Security requirements. Bea offers them something to eat before they head to Casa Oscar Romero.

Just as authorities ring the doorbell, I get a call from a young woman asking what we are most in need of. "Thank you so much. I'm sorry. We're a little busy right now. Would you mind calling back tomorrow?" I say.

Welcoming so many families—mainly couples with young children—gives me a taste of what daily life is like in the other houses. At least our new guests arrive in the afternoon and not at 9 p.m.

Several families will be traveling to Boston. We have a small supply of donated coats, sweaters, hats, and gloves to offer guests who are traveling to cold climates.

A Presbyterian congregation brings dinner every Monday evening. That helps so much, particularly today since we have so many new people. After phone calls and travel arrangements are made, all the new people move on by the end of the day. Two volunteers meet upstairs to prepare for five BAE groups scheduled for January.

Our director meets here with a candidate for mayor and is interviewed by a local TV station. Ruben does a great job with the media.

DECEMBER 3, 2019

Ruben meets a family from Mexico on the bridge. They have been turned back twice because the detention center is "full," which is, evidently, not the case. After he makes a few phone calls, the family is allowed through.

Today we are preparing to welcome nineteen people, families from Mexico and Guatemala. We regularly see the impact of cartels, violence, and extortion in certain Mexican states like Guerrero, Michoacán, and Zacatecas. Over half of the new arrivals are on a bus by evening, heading to their sponsors. All will have their day in court and may or may not be allowed to make a permanent home in the U.S.

I am tickled to see those staying overnight enjoying their first taste of pumpkin pie and ice cream, including an adorable one-year-old who ate her fair share.

Maybe it's because I'm still new at this, but I feel the tears rising as I walk people to the bus station or watch their driver pull away after a hug and a blessing. It's clear that they are also moved by the respect and kindness they have received here. It reminds me of my time as a hospital chaplain: You make a heart connection with people while they are in your care, and then you let them go. Some get back in touch later, or we hear their news from other guests. For most, we never learn what happens.

This is my most intense day so far.

DECEMBER 4, 2019

I need a few hours to myself this morning. I hop on one of the old streetcars. The originals were brought here from San Diego when the service was started up again. You can ride for no charge.

There's no charge to ride these vintage streetcars in El Paso.

I TAKE a stroll through the UTEP campus. I've been wanting to go to the Centennial Museum to see "Uncaged Art," an exhibit of pieces created by the kids in cages at the infamous tent city in Tornillo that served as a temporary detention facility.

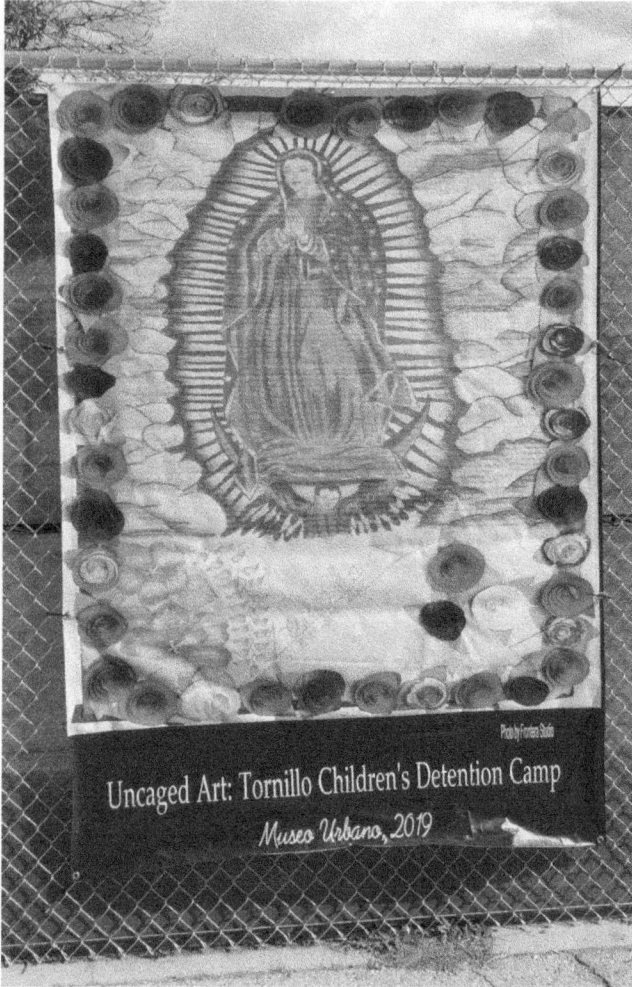

A moving exhibit of children's art from the Tornillo detention facility.

THE EXHIBIT MAKES a connection between the children and the quetzal, the multi-colored bird with the long tail feathers who cannot live without freedom. When caged, the quetzal dies.

The quetzal bird cannot live in captivity.

THERE IS enough time to visit the little hand-built temple from Bhutan. It is open for a tour.

The outing ends with a stop at the Coffee Box, a coffee shop built from shipping containers across from San Jacinto Plaza.

DECEMBER 5, 2019

A mom who left a few days ago calls to express her heartfelt thanks. This work inspires me to imagine a world where life can thrive again, and respect and mutual care are the cultural foundation for our life together.

Because of the longevity of the organization, our director gets many requests for interviews. A reporter from ABC-7 asked Ruben if the lowest point of the year was when an immigrant man was accused of assaulting an immigrant woman.

"'Not so,' Ruben said. 'I'll tell you what to me personally the low point was: it was August the third [and the mass shooting]. And that was the low point because we had an incident. We had an event where someone from out of town came into our community and specifically targeted people who were different, Mexicans and Hispanics. And to me that very much meant the refugee, the immigrant.'

"Before that shooting rampage, Ruben held frequent press briefings, updating news organizations about the latest numbers and the dynamics of the people affected. But that communication was suddenly cut off.

"'I cannot help but ask myself, had this individual been aware that there were hospitality houses for refugees, might he have gone there instead of Walmart?' said Garcia".[1]

MOST PEOPLE ARRIVE with only the clothes on their backs. Even their shoes are taken away in detention. It is winter here, but many come to us wearing black patent flip flops instead of shoes.

Tom Kiefer, a janitor and photographer, has become known for his photo collages of items Border Patrol agents have taken away from those apprehended: wallets, combs and brushes, toothpaste tubes, rosaries, condoms, shoelaces, clothing, and toys. There are many ways to rob people of their dignity and sense of belonging.

DECEMBER 6, 2019

During the week, after breakfast, we usually go upstairs to the volunteer room to begin the day with a check-in and a reflection. It's helpful to share how we are doing in the moment with the joys and challenges of the work. Then, whoever is on shift brings a poem, a reading, a video, or a question for discussion. It sets a tone for the day. If there's any business that needs discussion, we do that afterward.

There is no reflection this morning, though, after a water pipe bursts upstairs. I walk into the great room to find guests and staff mopping up an inch or so of water. I grab a mop. The problem is quickly isolated, and we're all dry now!

DECEMBER 7, 2019

It is my first time crossing the Paso del Norte bridge into Mexico—with a passport this time! I'm with friends, Betty, Peter, and Dave. I was invited to spend last night and today in Juárez at Casa Tabor, Peter and Betty's modest home on a mesa west of downtown.

Their property is a rental, in ruins when they moved in. They negotiated permission to do anything they wanted with the place in return for three years' free rent. The fence around the property is made of wooden pallets, intentionally low so potential robbers can easily see there is nothing of value. People say there are fewer break-ins when houses display an image of the Lady of Guadalupe.

There is a lot of lively conversation after a first look at El Paso's much larger sister city. Like many of the people I am meeting in the community, Peter and Betty served for many years in Latin America —in their case, Peru.

Casa Tabor in Juárez, Mexico.

Peter, at age ninety-six, still treks back and forth across the bridge once a week to attend the Border Peace Presence to witness against war, violence, and injustice. He is an Army veteran and a Carmelite priest. Betty is a former nurse who once drew blood from the arms of Plowshares anti-nuclear activists, blood they would later splatter on the walls of nuclear weapons facilities. She is a Sister of Mercy who hosts a quarterly women's group. Dave is a Carmelite brother who is an old friend of Peter and Betty.

Betty shows me the memorial to truth, justice, peace, and love that she maintains behind Casa Tabor. It honors the murdered and disappeared. There is a column for the 304 journalists killed in Mexico since 1993, priests killed in Mexico since 1990, some of the women and some of the men killed in Ciudad Juárez, along with some of the disappeared. There is a column for those who died in the U.S. desert since 2005—around half were unidentified. It's deeply unsettling to bear witness to this level of violence.

The four of us: (from left) Dave, Peter, Betty and the author.

"To live with lies is exhausting.
To speak the truth has consequences.
This is the price people have paid for their moral courage."
—Ruben Garcia

DECEMBER 8, 2019

On the way back to El Paso, I hesitate to take photos of the tent city at the entrance to the bridge in Juárez. It's easy to exploit vulnerable people. The side street near the bridge is where families have been camping out. Dave and I speak briefly with a man from Honduras who has been there with his family for the past two months. There are shelters and assistance in Juárez, but it is a far more dangerous situation, according to people I talk to.

Children living on the streets in a Juárez tent city.

I'm back at the house in time for our all-volunteer reflection time, where we remember the six children who have died in U.S. custody.

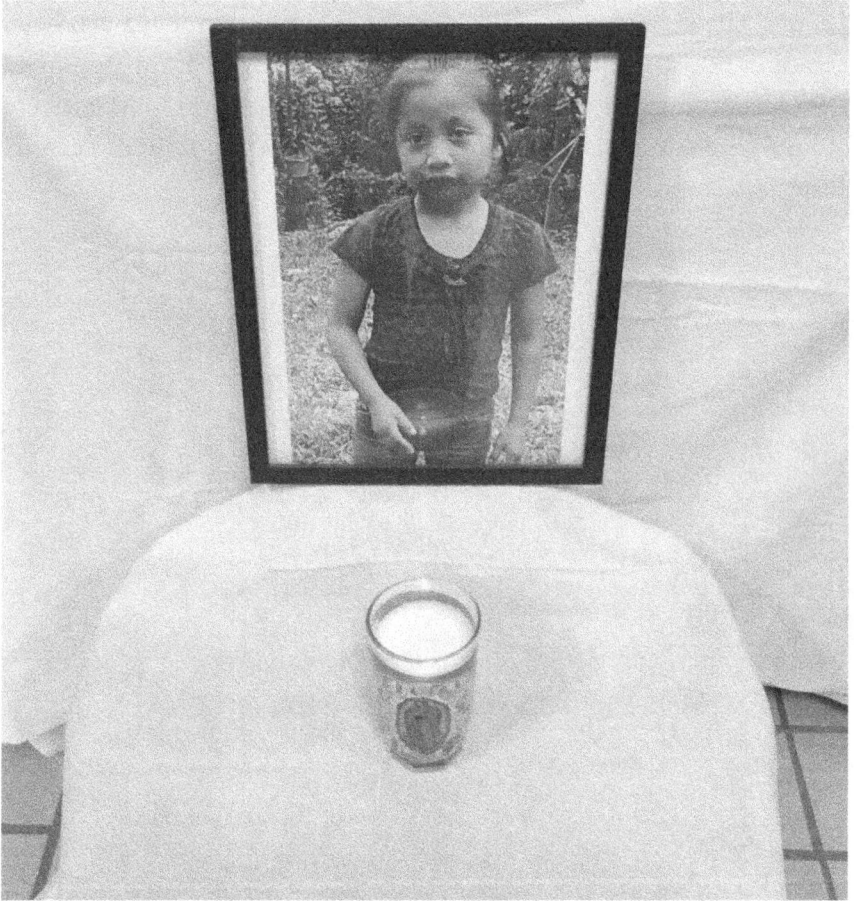

Jakelin Caal Maquin, an Indigenous child from Guatemala, died at age seven in U.S. custody.

On this day one year ago, Jakelin Caal Maquin died at age seven. She was an Indigenous child from Guatemala. Her death was the first. Jakelin's father was not permitted to accompany his daughter en route to Providence Children's Hospital here in El Paso, but he was allowed to be with her as she was dying. He was a guest at Annunciation House for several months. I remember when little Jakelin's death was in the news. She and her story have haunted me since then. I am grateful her memory is honored in this way.

DECEMBER 10, 2019

It's 10 p.m. and I am winding down before another intense day tomorrow. It was also a full week last week as our quiet home suddenly became much livelier.

Last Monday, we received fourteen guests for short-term stays. On Tuesday, we received another nineteen, including a father and son from Cuba who had been granted asylum. Their three attorneys were so happy with the ruling, unusual in El Paso. They had a hard time saying goodbye. Many of the new people departed on their bus the same day they arrived.

On Sunday, two long-term families were assigned to us, making five families in total now. We have nine children, including two infants.

This is more activity compressed into a short time than I've seen so far. And it's nothing compared to the wave of humanity the other houses deal with every day—and nothing compared to the peak last summer when 500 to 600 people were released by authorities every day. But the other houses don't deal with school enrollments, vaccinations, and medical check-ups. Boredom for long-term guests may be the biggest challenge in our house.

I'm content with my assignment here. I like getting to know the guests. We laugh a lot as the Spanish speakers try out their English, and I gain confidence in my Spanish. I even got a compliment today from someone who noticed the improvement.

———

So much for winding down...

It is nearly midnight with temperatures in the forties. Someone is tapping on my door. I want to ignore it. It is Rosaleen asking for help. It was she who heard the doorbell.

After getting dressed, I find two moms and two young people shivering in the great room. They have just crossed the river and the irrigation canal. The girl is getting over a case of chickenpox. I'm not sure how they found us, but they spent their only money on a taxi.

I hurry downstairs to gather blankets for them to wrap up in. Rosaleen finds dry clothes for them. While they shower, I heat up leftovers and set the table.

Now, they are warm and comfortable. Our director has been notified. The new guests ask if they can help with the dishes.

"Tomorrow," I say, "not tonight."

A small room upstairs is waiting for them. Hopefully, we'll all get some sleep now.

DECEMBER 11, 2019

This morning, I take two families to enroll their children in the local elementary school. The kids are given a backpack, school supplies, and a uniform including socks and shoes—all donated by the community.

I like going to the school in person rather than registering the kids online. It takes a good hour and a half to guide the parents through forms and more forms and choices. It's exhausting for everyone.

One of the questions parents have to answer is whether they are living in a private home, temporary housing, a shelter, or are homeless. That question makes me grow cold inside, and it's important information for teachers and counselors to have.

DECEMBER 12, 2019

Today is my day off.

It is also the feast day of the beloved Lady of Guadalupe. I'd heard so much about the lively and passionate festivities in Juárez with mariachis and processions, but I don't make it there.

I sleep. A lot. Then I walk a few miles to enjoy a delectable lunch at Cafe Mayapan, a project of *La Mujer Obrera*—The Working Woman. This organization focuses on reclaiming Indigenous culture, economic development, community-building, health, and civic engagement. I order tortilla soup, bean and red onion tostadas, and a cool drink generically called *agua fresca,* ladled Mexican-style from a large jar.

Cafe Mayapan

From there, I take the bus back downtown, get a library card, and take home one of three books Betty insisted I read: *Storming the Wall: Climate Change, Migration, and Homeland Security*. The book will help me gain insight into how my work at the border relates to the initiatives on water and energy I've been involved with at home.

Our household continues to expand. Bea gets permission for one of the Mexican women she knows to stay here along with her son, instead of going to Casa Oscar Romero. Julia is here for a month to fulfill the Social Security requirement. She will help us manage the cooking and cleanup assignments. Her son is in high school. He is also an asset. He's already taught our junior high schooler to play chess. The latter was aggressive with the younger children at times early on in his stay. He didn't want to leave his home country and was understandably angry. With the structure of school and support from volunteers and guests, he is becoming happier and more self-confident.

Since my arrival, I've been on a mission to convince my colleagues to ditch the abundance of nonstick pots and pans that have been bleeding PFAS and PFOA, the forever chemicals, into the water and into our bodies. Most of the pans were hand-me-downs with bottoms and sides worn down to bare metal.

My colleagues are eager to participate and probably also want to keep an eye on me. We also get rid of other things we aren't using. After that, we relax over tea and banana bread.

It will take time to replace some of the cookware. I feel tension in the air later as staff and guests can't find their favorite pan.

Ironically, Sandy, a volunteer at one of the other houses, invites me to see the documentary, *Dark Waters*, this evening. It's the true story of the attorney who worked to hold DuPont accountable for knowingly contaminating the water of a town in West Virginia with these chemicals.

Michigan has the most documented PFAS contamination of any

state in the country. A friend who lives just five miles from me learned that his well is highly contaminated. It was announced yesterday that Wolverine Worldwide will pay $69.5 million in a PFAS settlement. These "forever chemicals" accumulate in the body and do not break down over time.[2]

The pots and pans...safer now!

DECEMBER 13, 2019

We see many families coming from the Mexican states of Guerrero, Michoacán, and Zacatecas where cartels have become powerful and vicious. Extortion is one of their weapons.

Imagine: You have a successful business and a family. You've been approached by a cartel for a third time. Every time they have demanded a larger payment. You tell them you don't have the money. They threaten to kill your children. You know they mean it.

You pack up your car and your family that night. You head for the border to ask for asylum. You call a neighbor and ask them to keep an eye on your house. U.S. authorities are required to let you in because you are from Mexico. If you had come from another country, you would be put into the MPP and sent back across the border to wait your turn where conditions are dangerous.

Your family is put in detention for several days. After what you've been through, it's hard to understand why. You end up at Casa Vides. You call home to see if your neighbor will send you some essential documents. They tell you your home has been ransacked. There is nothing left.

Looking for work is prohibited while you are in the process. Your car insurance is due, and you can't pay the bill. Your car is now uninsured.

What do you do?

DECEMBER 14, 2019

We have many skilled cooks in the house. All this goodness often includes handmade tortillas!

Making tortillas by hand.

Yesterday, the volunteer staff discussed how much the house has changed and what needs to change as a result. We all agreed we were having difficulties meeting more than the most basic needs of our guests, where everyone is dealing with much uncertainty, anxiety, and trauma from the journey north.

Imagine having your extended family coming for an indefinite visit! Your relatives are coming from different countries and contexts, and none of you have ever met before. Children outnumber parents.

Bea calls a *junta*, a meeting of everyone in the house. The families are invited to share frustrations and needs. It really clears the air.

We've gone from two families to seven in less than a week—and from six children to eleven, one probably on the autism spectrum. It's been pretty demanding for all of us, especially with Chris away after a death in the family. He is the only one who is authorized to drive the house car, so I have to call on volunteer drivers in the community. It all takes time.

Everyone enjoys moments of calm after the kids are off to school. There is a minor uproar when they return home. Two of them are still at home. One is still recovering from chickenpox. The other was advised not to start school during exam week and have those grades on his record.

We're waiting for Danny, a doctor we can call on, to arrive to look at the two adults and two kids who crossed the river in the cold. He stops by after a long day in his own practice.

I spend many hours getting several adults enrolled in a free clinic that does not accept children.

"You can come in on Monday at 6:45 and wait."

"Can we come today and wait to see the doctor?"

"No, the doctor isn't here anymore."

"When can we make an appointment, so we don't need to wait?"

"You can't. We have installed new software, and that function isn't available yet."

"When will it be available?"

"We don't know, and we're as frustrated as you are."

I remind myself that navigating these systems is what people without financial resources deal with every day.

DECEMBER 15, 2019

This experience at the U.S./Mexico border feels like a dress rehearsal for something bigger. It is impossible for me to take in that one in ten of us may be displaced and on the move as the climate continues to destabilize.

In *Storming the Wall,* Todd Miller writes: "Just like super-typhoons, rising seas, and heat waves, border build-up and militarization are by-products of climate change... If nothing changes we will find ourselves living in an increasingly militarized world of surveillance, razor wire, border walls, armed patrols, detention centers, and relocation camps...not only [in] the United States but throughout the planet, where more securitized borders divide the Global North and Global South than ever before."[3]

There are no legal protections for people seeking refuge from climate change. These people will not necessarily be from other lands. Where will all the people from Miami and other coastal cities in the U.S. go as sea levels continue to rise? The U.S. remains the largest historical emitter of the greenhouse gasses that are trapping heat in the atmosphere.[4] While China now holds the top spot for these emissions, my comfortable way of life is still implicated because China has become the leading offshore manufacturer for this country.[5] The harms already done to climate stability and global temperatures are irreversible. Some future changes are unavoidable but can be limited. Sometimes it takes a crisis to open our eyes. A climate stable enough to grow food can no longer be assumed in a growing number of places. Africa, Asia, and Central and South America are already feeling the pain. Africa has contributed the least to this destabilization, accounting for less than 4% of global greenhouse gas emissions.[6] It's a profound injustice.

DECEMBER 16, 2019

"Are you making that for the Guadalupe?" our six-year-old asks me expectantly this morning. I am cutting up fruit for salad for a dinner we are hosting at the house.

"Yes, I am," I tell her. She looks very pleased.

Our Lady of Guadalupe holds so much meaning for many of those who stay with us at Casa Vides.

DECEMBER 17, 2019

I call it nailing jello to the wall...

I am gradually taking on more responsibilities, and most every day is filled with things I am doing for the first time. Focusing on anything until it's done is always a challenge. Frequent interruptions are the norm in a shelter.

Today, I start the process of getting a copy of my driving record so I can be added to the insurance policy for the house car. We have many community drivers to call on, but it takes time making calls to see who is free.

Our ten-month-old was running a fever again last night, and Mom wants the doctor to stop by for a second exam. Before coming to us, the little one had been hospitalized for pneumonia. I leave a message for Danny who always finds a way to fit us in and is always reminding us we should never hesitate to call.

While I am away, he returns the call and is told the baby is much better. Then the fever starts again. Mom is confused about why the doctor didn't come.

I call Danny again. He will call in a prescription, but can't stop by until 8 p.m. Bea takes a poll. Who else needs to see the doctor? It seems like most of us have a cough or a sore throat, passing our germs back and forth. Our three-year-old, who threw up on the dining room floor this morning and developed an ugly cough, was treated.

Tina, an Episcopal priest and a friend of the house, stops by before dinner and offers to pick up the antibiotics after a long day in Juárez. She runs an informal school for children whose families are living on the street. She waits until 9 p.m. for a prescription we were told would be ready by 7 p.m.

This is how we nail jello to the wall here at Casa Vides.

DECEMBER 18, 2019

Every month, the volunteers at each house are encouraged to take a community day to relax, have some fun, and get to know each other better. My colleagues here claim that they haven't managed to go out on one of these mini-adventures all year. Today is going to be the day...well, the afternoon, at least.

Our plan is to visit an eco-home and women's center run by a small group of Indigenous sisters in a barrio called Lomas de Poleo in Anapra, Mexico.

Tonantzin, the women's center in Lomas de Poleo, Anapra, Mexico.

"Have you heard?" Bea asks me after lunch. "Rosaleen says 226 people will be released today. Ruben asked if we could take sixteen of them."

I can only imagine the look on my face. I can't imagine Bea saying no. But she did in a very diplomatic way. Kathy, our new community volunteer, will cover for us. One person can't handle so many people on their own.

Our "Commy Day" is so interesting and fun. One of the sisters drives to the bridge to pick us up. Many of the dirt roads are so rugged and washed out that our car has to proceed very slowly to our destination. People in Anapra often live without plumbing. On the outskirts of town going up the mountain, people live in dwellings constructed of cardboard. They can see the lights and skyline of El Paso at night, the logos of banks and hotels on the tallest buildings.

The grounds are an oasis of calm and order in the midst of dire poverty. The place is surrounded by the hills the barrio is named for, with the grand sweep of the mountains in the distance.

Our hosts are gracious and warm. Their home is full of natural light and designed to not require heating or air-conditioning. They use composting toilets. On the grounds is an herb and vegetable garden and young fruit trees. The women's center next door is named after Tonantzin, a Nahuatl title meaning something like "our ancient venerable mother." Tonantzin comes from the Aztec tradition. Some say she represents Mother Earth herself. The image of Our Lady of Guadalupe appears next to the name of the center, two names and faces honoring the sacred feminine principle, melding Indigenous and Christian culture.

We end the day by taking the sister who is our chauffeur out to dinner before walking back across the bridge. She chooses *La Nueva Central*, a sort of Carnegie Deli, Mexican-style, in the heart of downtown Juárez. The meal for all five of us, including dessert, costs around $21.

Restaurant La Nueva Central in downtown Juárez.

DECEMBER 18, 2019

I give my first introduction and house tour to a BAE group. It's their first full day. While they'll get no academic credit for the experience, it is clearly life-changing for many. These guests are all students at universities in Chicago. I am impressed by their questions.

My first time doing a house tour for *a Border Awareness Experience* group.

DECEMBER 19, 2019

She fell after climbing and falling from the border wall. Her brother and her two children, three-years and ten-months-old, were unharmed. After a visit to the hospital, she comes to us in a wheel-chair with her children.

DECEMBER 20, 2019

I have an hour or so to visit El Paso's Holocaust museum.

I read that in 1938, around 17,000 Jewish people were expelled from Germany to Poland. They were refused entry and had to walk back and forth between the two countries until they were allowed in and permitted to live in ghettos.

That's eerily similar to what's been happening in the Mediterranean, at the wall between India and Bangladesh, and here at the U.S./Mexico border.

DECEMBER 22, 2019

The *posada* is a Latin American tradition, a reenactment of a Jewish couple's search for a place to rest, far away from home before the birth of their child, Yeshua of Nazareth. It's taking place this evening in the Duranguito. Miriam rides on a donkey with Yosef leading the way. The figures are drawn slowly through the barrio on a cart. They are coldly turned away with songs twice by those who don't want to be bothered, claiming they have no room.

The posada celebrates the journey of Miriam and Yosef, a metaphor for all people who seek shelter and are turned away.

The third stop on the posada's route is Casa Vides. The door opens wide and everyone is welcomed inside for a celebration. We are only playing a role in this annual ritual. For our guests, it is their lived experience.

Our families are introduced to the other participants and offered encouragement. A spontaneous collection is taken up after the visitors learn of the surprisingly steep bus fare needed by the woman who fell from the wall a few days ago, her two young children, and the friend who had come for them this afternoon. This friend had already opened her home to our guest's sister and her two older children. There were tears of gratitude.

Our injured guest leaves in a wheelchair with one leg in a cast, wearing a body brace. Several of the families and two of our volunteers walk the travelers to the bus station a few blocks away and wait with them for a time.

My first posada makes for a powerful evening. It couldn't be more relevant for these times. This casual spirit of generosity and common cause that flowed so naturally after the ritual...well...this feels like the world I'd like to live in.

DECEMBER 22, 2019

Today was supposed to be my first two days off in a row. Instead, all the volunteers are going to Juárez. I've been wondering about what kind of presence is planned for Annunciation House across the border where the needs are so great. We'll get to see today, and we're excited.

Many say it is preferable to be in detention because of the conditions and the violence in Mexican border cities. There are shelters and services available in Juárez, but not enough to meet current realities.

There will be not one, but three houses. We get to see the two in Juárez. The third, the straw bale house in Anapra that was closed during the years of extreme violence, will reopen.

Annunciation House Juárez will be staffed by experienced volunteers. Casa Guadalupe will provide transitional housing to Central American women and their children. It will not be staffed. In Anapra, Casa Emmaus will focus on two-parent families. Temperatures dipped to below freezing last night. These shelters will help meet some of the immediate need. There is also much good work being done by so many groups and individuals.

DECEMBER 23, 2019

They were a group from two troubled Central American countries. They found their way to Juárez where they were kidnapped and tortured for several weeks before being trafficked to El Paso. They are now at our big house, CDR. A volunteer therapist has been enlisted and has already begun some group work with them.

We will receive another injured guest who came over the border wall tomorrow after her release from hospital.

DECEMBER 24, 2019

It is Christmas Eve day. The injured individual does not arrive, but we receive two other guests today, a mom and her two-day-old baby.

The kitchen is crowded from morning to night. Making tamales is a traditional labor-intensive project this time of year. The children are all home on semester break. Visitors are in and out. Volunteers are in and out. Donations come in. The phone rings a lot. I am on shift and can't find time for a break.

For me, Christmas is a complicated holiday. There are so many expectations that make for stress. My preference is to respect the religious aspects of the holiday for those who follow a Christian path. Children love the excitement of their gifts, but I wonder what lessons they are being taught, especially the children getting their first introduction to the holiday as it is celebrated here.

BEFORE: Our kids' corner is a place to find toys, books, puzzles, and art supplies. The material we store there encourages sharing, creativity, reading, problem-solving made fun, and working together. The TV in the great room is used to watch movies. We have a small library of family-oriented DVDs. No one seems to get tired of the magic and lessons of *Coco*, including me. Out back there are tricycles, balls, and such. Free movies have been showing at the beautiful Plaza Theater on weekends all month.

AFTER: Waves of plastic toys began to flood in last week. They came from the elementary school, from a group of police officers who arrived on bicycles with Santa Claus hats, and from events at WinterFest. Many are big, battery-powered, and noisy with flashing lights. Some are remote-controlled. The children are captivated for a while. Beige and brown girls carry around blonde, blue-eyed Barbies. Given that apprehensions reflect daily life at the border and the recent experiences of some of our guests, the most ironic game that comes into the house this season involves handcuffs. The kids are intrigued. The game includes physical handcuffs and keys. It is surreal to watch the kids play at arresting each other. It always leads to quarrels and mayhem.

I look forward to the slow return of the light after the winter solstice. I appreciate the quiet anticipation of Advent, the simplicity of Hanukkah and the principles of Kwanzaa. Most of all, I like to be still during this season as the land and many of her creatures begin a long slumber. I appreciate the time to reflect on the gifts of the year that is ending and write out my intentions for the year to come.

One evening, I rode the streetcar home after an outing. At one of the stops, three men in Army fatigues and Santa hats got on with their instruments and began to play "Joy to the World." Meanwhile, we hear and see helicopters patrolling the border every day. Meanwhile, families shiver under tarps on the south side of the Paso del Norte bridge with temperatures below freezing. Meanwhile, women are struggling to get out of abusive situations at home on this side of the bridge. Hollow-eyed men hang out near the Greyhound station. The needs are so great. What we invest ourselves in is such a mashup.

On weekends, there is entertainment at WinterFest and a small skating rink nearby. San Jacinto Plaza is a lively gathering place filled with families strolling around and enjoying themselves. Our guests can easily walk there from the house.

I AM HOPING my offer to stay home while everyone gathers for another posada, Mass, and dinner at the big house will be accepted. The new guest and her three-day-old infant need to be accompanied to the bus station in the evening. And we are still expecting the hospital to release someone who fell after scaling the border wall. I need some quiet time and get my wish.

DECEMBER 25, 2019

A friend shares a powerful image of an immigrant family with golden halos walking alone through a desert landscape. It juxtaposes the situation here at the border with the Christian nativity story that most people from Latin America would claim as theirs. What would shift if we could see every family as worthy of respect, support, and care?

Our volunteer team agrees that the toy situation is getting out of hand. We organize a simple celebration that doesn't involve more toys. We ask the parents to keep the kids in their rooms until 9 a.m. We rise early enough to enjoy coffee, sweet bread, and some leisurely conversation. Then, we go from room to room singing *Feliz Navidad* accompanied by Chris on the guitar. Most of the guests love it.

I asked earlier if one of the volunteers would be willing to say a few things to our families when we gather. It's been frustrating to not be able to communicate in Spanish beyond the basics. Instead, they give me the opportunity and assign a translator in case my words fail.

I want our guests to know that they have been blessings to us and that we are so grateful to have them here. I want them to know that we understand that they are dealing with so much: sorrow, loss, trauma for some, separation from loved ones, fear, uncertainty, financial difficulties, and more. We don't know how long we'll all be together, and it's not always easy. But for now, we are a family, sharing moments of joy and laughter in the midst of it all. Everyone receives a small fleece blanket to snuggle up with on cold desert nights.

The moms decide what they want to make for brunch and start cooking. Chris makes pancake batter with the children. The boys need his example so badly, one in particular. They follow him around adoringly and ask for him often when he is away. He takes them all out to a park for soccer practice after the meal.

I enjoy the day.

DECEMBER 27, 2019

Tomorrow, one of the volunteers is loaning me her car so I can get out of town for my first two-day break. Ahhh....

Reminders of militarized borders are difficult to leave behind. I have my first experience with a checkpoint. I am waved through. Motorists have to pass through checkpoints like this on all major highways leading away from the border, often a hundred miles inland. Border Patrol agents are also boarding trains and keeping an eye out at bus stations and other locations in major cities.

White Sands National Park in New Mexico is a vast expanse of gypsum sand dunes between the grand sweep of the San Andreas and Sacramento Mountains.

I am visiting the White Sands National Park in New Mexico, a vast expanse of gypsum sand dunes between the grand sweep of the San Andreas and Sacramento Mountains. They are on the ancestral lands of a number of tribal nations, most recently the Mescalero Apache. I wish I could have an Apache elder as a guide.

The gypsum dunes are so much easier to walk on than sand dunes. The sand is only loose on the surface and never gets hot in summer. Dig down a way and you'll find water, though it's too salty to drink. White moths, lizards, and mice have adapted themselves to blend in with the expanses of whiteness.

I have missed being able to walk on the land.

By the afternoon, my shoulders drop, and I realize I'm feeling very relaxed as I walk around Las Cruces and Mesilla. I have some interesting conversations. There won't be enough time to walk at Dripping Springs. The sky is darkening. Somehow I miss seeing the twenty-foot-tall roadrunner sculpture made entirely of trash near the I-10 on the drive home.

DECEMBER 28, 2019

The military, Border Patrol, ICE, and other government agencies maintain a high profile in the area. Here are a few examples from my getaway.

Fort Bliss. I drive by this vast installation as I leave El Paso. "In addition to the dynamic mountain terrain, Fort Bliss also claims a staggering 1.2 million acres of desert outfitted for training, replete with dozens of mock villages and cities...

"El Pasoans are generally friendly with a gracious attitude towards the abundant military, federal, and government workers that make up a significant slice of the region's workforce and economy. The DEA, U.S. Customs and Border Patrol, the FBI, and many other agencies have offices in El Paso.

"Plans to build a detention center for 1,000 unaccompanied young people, with the possibility of expanding to 7,000, are stalled for the moment. The base is riddled with toxic hazards including unexploded munitions. The U.S. military is said to be the largest polluter and one of the largest emitters of greenhouse gasses.

"Fort Bliss also interned people during WWII. The historical record indicates that while the Fort Bliss internment camp housed primarily male detainees, a number of those Japanese male internees, whose families were left destitute by the internment of the head of their households, were joined by spouses and children prior to November 1942 and the closing of [the station]." [7]

I go through another checkpoint. I see a border patrol agent and a dog walking not far from the road. I'd just begun to feel like I had left the borderlands behind. A converted weigh station is now a checkpoint on the northbound side. There are a flock of cameras on the southbound side. We are all waved through.

"I thought it was strange at first, then I got used to it," said a woman originally from Ohio who had moved to the area.

Checkpoints are marked on maps. People tell me they have been operational for decades. They were closed for four months earlier this year when personnel were diverted to the border due to the large influx of people asking for asylum. They reopened in August.

I see a sheriff's vehicle and a group of officers looking for something or someone just before Alamogordo, New Mexico. There is a Customs and Border Protection station there.

Holloman Air Force Base lies just to the east of the White Sands National Park. White Sands Missile Range is west of the park. It's the largest military installation in the U.S. The first atomic bomb was detonated as a test near the northern boundary of the range in 1945.

DECEMBER 29, 2019

Last week, the house van had a flat tire. This was not surprising considering the construction going on next door.

Chris went to a garage to get the tire repaired, but the nail went in near the wall of the tire.

"Sorry. We can't repair it," the mechanic says. "It's the law."

He had to buy a new tire.

One of our guests used to be a mechanic. When he hears the story, he smiles and asks, "Where do you think all those tires go? Honduras." Then he tells us about the tool they use to repair these tires. "Not a problem," he says.

DECEMBER 31, 2019

My New Year's Eve day begins with a sweet moment, helping our often cantankerous three-year-old pull on his socks and overalls. Some young people from the community bring us a yummy breakfast of small, homemade burritos.

The used shoe dealer on the corner has started to give us practical shoes when we run short of a particular size. So we return the favor. Two of us take him a box and a big bag of donated shoes: large, expensive men's shoes, hiking boots, and some women's four-inch stilettos that don't work for our guests. Tidying up the basement clothes closet, linen room, shop, pharmacy, pantry, and craft supplies is a project we're focusing on right now. Another BAE group arrives on Sunday. We'll host four groups in January, and they'll spend time downstairs in the evenings.

LIVING in a shelter is a bit surreal sometimes. You never know what scene will be unfolding in the living room. Before heading out for a haircut, I find most of the kids and our house coordinator jumping around the living room with an exercise video.

When you've been living in a place long enough to need a haircut, you must be settling in. My besties at the house assure me that D-Elsa's, just a ten-minute walk from the house, is the place to go. Much of El Paso looks like a typical American city. But the closer you get to the border, the more shops, like D-Elsa's, look like the ones in Mexico. The historic segundo barrio is called "The Other Ellis Island" because so many people immigrate through the area.

When I return, our ten-month-old is in her high chair sitting like a queen in front of the television, watching a movie with the others.

D-Elsa's is the place we go when we need a haircut.

After cleaning up after the evening meal that featured a Honduran specialty dish, we gather in a circle in the living room to sing familiar songs from our different homes. One of the young people practices his breakdancing. Our only couple gets up and starts to dance. Singing the old songs brings tears to the eyes of several guests. Some have been staying in their rooms with their children most of the day and find it difficult to be a part of meals and activities. If they come for a time, they leave early. It's too much. So it's particularly nice to have everyone present.

After that, it is *piñata* time. One of our guests climbs up on a ladder and tosses the piñata around to make it more challenging for the older kids. There are two piñatas. One is traditional. The other is a bird. Our six-year-old puts her arms around the creature before the others begin to tear it to shreds with a decorated stick.

As you can imagine, the excitement of piñatas and candy gets young people stirred up. Two come inside, each brandishing a long piece of PVC pipe with one of the bird's feet at the end. This looks like trouble.

I have an art project prepared to settle everyone down for bed, but the parents whisk their children off to their rooms. We volunteers stay up to greet the new year, ending the day upstairs with a dish of mint chocolate chip ice cream.

JANUARY 2020

There are stories I have heard that I do not share because they are deeply disturbing. This one is difficult enough. This individual has chosen to share her story in public.

She shows me the newspaper articles today. They were printed a few years ago after her mother was murdered, leaving behind six children. The articles include her mother's photo and describe what happened to her that day in broad daylight. The family does not know who is responsible: a cartel, a gang, or someone else. I come across an article in a publication in the Irish Times with this headline: "Anyone can murder a woman in Honduras and nothing will happen."

The young person who shared the articles has her own story. She was raped when she was barely old enough to conceive her first child. The man was prosecuted and convicted, which is quite unusual in her country. He is out of prison now. The family headed north together. Now they are scattered. One sister decided to stay in

Mexico. Her brother is working on the other side of the border. Her three younger siblings live in a nonprofit facility for minors in Arizona. Our guest is here on her own with three children, including an infant. She has no sponsor.

JANUARY 3, 2020

This is our backyard. There is a picnic table and plenty of room for the children to play. El Paso is located in the vast Chihuahuan Desert. We get sand and dust in our eyes when it's windy. There are no dryers in the house and the clotheslines are almost always full. The sheets carry that fresh scent of sunshine.

The back yard at Casa Vides.

JANUARY 4, 2020

The new semester begins on Wednesday. I think it's safe to say that both parents and volunteers are looking forward to a lower decibel level during the day.

Until today, it's been too cold for the kids to burn off some of that boundless energy outside. Art projects, such as drawing hopes and dreams for the new year, keep them occupied for hours.

I have a full week ahead with enrollments, vaccinations, and doctor's appointments. I'm still waiting to be added to the insurance policy for the house vehicle. Lining up drivers adds a layer of detail to each day.

Temperatures are comfortable now during the day, but still dip regularly to below freezing at night.

The mountains in the distance are the Sierra de Juárez across the border in Mexico.

JANUARY 6, 2020

We know that some of our guests use *coyotes* or smugglers on their journey to the border. How this works is well understood on the street. If you can pay, shadowy figures will work to get you across the border. We learn that a pair of unaccompanied teens from Guatemala were dumped off at an unoccupied house, or stash house, in Juárez. From there, they crossed the river on their own. The parents of the twins live off the land in conditions of extreme poverty. They probably sacrificed everything they had to hire a coyote for their boys. After these young people receive some counsel from an attorney, they decide to turn themselves in to the authorities. (Our houses do not provide shelter to unaccompanied young people under age 18.)

We also know that once in the U.S., people use coyotes to get to where they want to go. Stash houses that were used in Pancho Villa's day to hide cash and valuables, now house human beings between segments of their journey.

While we abide by the law, it's not our role to parent or police. That means we do not get involved in any way with coyotes.

Coyotes have a financial interest in encouraging people to come north. For that reason, they do not give the best advice on the risks and dangers. Some cheat, abuse, or abandon their clients.

Smugglers are part of border culture. It's a business. Coyotes are used to adapting to changing conditions. Checkpoints have also been in place for decades. The screws are tightening, and the expense is dizzying. Cartels will resort to whatever means necessary to continue to operate. In fact, cartels in some states in Mexico and other places are becoming more vicious and demanding.

Increasingly militarized borders are actually helping cartels and the underworld they bring with them grow more powerful. They also make conditions much more dangerous for those determined to seek entry into one of the wealthier countries. My understanding is still quite limited, but it's something that has been on my mind.

JANUARY 8, 2020

It's taking a long time to be authorized to drive the house vehicle.

The day begins with a 9 a.m. doctor's exam for our little guy. It's required by his preschool program. The driver shows up promptly at 8:30 a.m. I ride along with the family. When Annunciation House was flooded with people some months ago, he says he often drove people to the airport. Sure enough, just a few minutes before 9 a.m., we are pulling into the airport! Oops.

When we arrive at the doctor's office, they have no record of an appointment and have no doctor named Hernandez on staff. It's the wrong office. On the third try, we are successful but arrive a half hour late. The staff say they will try to fit us in, but it takes the entire morning.

We arrive back home with ten minutes to spare before the next driver arrives. Mom drops off the three-year-old and collects the two-month-old for a well-baby exam. Of course, we have no diapers with us when that unmistakable smell wafts through the waiting room. Mercifully, another family with an infant donates to our cause. We will return in two weeks, as the baby is not meeting the norms for weight gain.

After a rest, I give a house tour for another BAE group, twenty-four students from two universities in Washington D.C. The dining room buzzes with lively conversations over dinner. The students love to interact with the guests. The children love to perform for them.

It's a long day.

JANUARY 9, 2020

I learn that Juárez and El Paso share an aquifer. That means cooperation on access to water as a source of life isn't optional.

JANUARY 10, 2020

It's another full day with a very full house at Casa Vides.

One BAE group from Minneapolis will leave tomorrow, and another group from Union Seminary in New York City will arrive. We'll have over fifty people for dinner on Friday evening. Our dining room can't hold many more.

The new guests don't arrive until 8:30 p.m. Of the three women, two are pregnant, including one who had contractions earlier in the day. She was seen at the children's hospital before she arrived. Our baby birthing workshop hasn't happened yet, so we are hoping for a calm night.

The large women's dorm is almost full. We juggle a few people around to create a smaller men's dorm.

Our director drops off a young person from Guatemala. Then he has a long conversation with one of the long-term families. The family now has a sponsor on the East Coast, the new community initiative by the BAE group that was here when I arrived. The family will be leaving in the next few weeks. They're relieved and joyful to finally have a plan and also sad to leave the unusual family we've become.

There have been more changes in policy that will continue to push the crisis further south and out of sight. More information is coming out about the DNA testing of people in the immigration system. One of the two pilots is underway in Detroit in my home state of Michigan.

JANUARY 11, 2020

I go by the longer version of my name here. It sounds beautiful in Spanish and is easier to pronounce: *Déborah*. One of the guests always speaks to me with mischief in her voice and eyes.

"*Déborah*, Pastor Rosemary has invited us to her church this afternoon. Is it okay for me to go?"

I feel a little jab in my heart, take a breath, and hope my Spanish is up to it. Only one of our guests can communicate in halting English. "Of course. You are free to go anywhere you want. We just appreciate knowing where you are."

We do have a few house rules and a sort of culture we all get used to. You're asked to wear shoes all the time. There's no eating in the bedrooms, because no one wants bugs in their bed. Curfew is at 9 p.m. and lights out is at 10 p.m. Let the volunteer in charge answer the door.

We are running a house of hospitality, not a detention center.

LAST WEEK, a man slit his throat on the bridge between two other border cities after being denied entry into the U.S.

The camps at the foot of the bridge in Juárez have been removed and people moved to shelters before the president of Mexico visits. The informal school Tina has been running has moved to another location.

People from Mexico and Central America seeking asylum in the U.S. are now being flown at taxpayer expense to Guatemala where they may apply for protection. Amazon co-owns Omni Air International, an airline that is involved in deportation flights and implicated in the alleged torture of its passengers.[1] Much of U.S. immigration policy seems focused on making life more difficult for people who already lead difficult lives.

JANUARY 12, 2020

Tina joins us for dinner this evening. I ask her if she thinks the visit by the president of Mexico provoked the sweep of the camps near the bridge or whether there was genuine concern about the cold snap's effects on families living under tarps.

She says she saw families threatened with having their children taken away if they refused to relocate to a shelter. People were given a short time to collect their things. Anything that remained was swept away as trash.

This sounds like the sweep of a homeless camp in Kalamazoo last year and the sweep of San Francisco before the Super Bowl.

People from Mexico have a legal right to cross the bridge and enter the U.S. to request asylum. With MPP, everyone else in theory is stopped. There is anecdotal evidence that people from Mexico are also being stopped from crossing.

Our director says, "Don't try to figure it out. You can't."

JANUARY 13, 2020

Always something. Our house coordinator fell and fractured a bone in her upper arm. It's not clear whether she will need surgery, but she's attending to everyone as usual with her arm in a sling.

JANUARY 14, 2020

Sometimes I color with the kids. Today I am marking the end of my second month here in El Paso. In these two months, I haven't been able to finish this page. Interruptions make it difficult to focus. My attention span has suffered.

There's also a feeling of lethargy that rises up in me at times. Long-term guests are here in a state of suspended animation. While people are grateful for the shelter and support, everyone finds themselves in a liminal space filled with uncertainty. They want to get on with their lives, and it's hard for them to see others moving on after just a few hours or a day.

Are there other things that sap my energies? I reflect on the "reality" I've been taught and accepted as normal. It's emotional and spiritual labor to begin to see through the interwoven stories we tell. Many don't quite match the realities I see and experience every day.

Coloring with the kids.

JANUARY 16, 2020

Helicopters on patrol are one of the first sounds I hear in the morning and one of the last at night. I can hear them now. Some days, it feels like we're living in a war zone. Some consider Border Patrol a growing paramilitary force that could be used on any of us in times of civil unrest. Police forces and the gear they use make them increasingly look like military troops.

THE FORM READS: "An ID is required to process your application. Please select one of the three groups and provide the required documents...Please note that all documents must be original, no copies will be accepted."

My latest challenge is to help one of our guests get a certified birth certificate for her infant who was born in El Paso a few months ago. The child will need a certified original in the future. I study the list of acceptable forms of identification by category on a website that is not available in Spanish and sigh with relief when I find my answer. Our guest can easily get a library card as a third form of identification. The main library is only a short walk away.

Documents and processes, rather than community and relationships of trust, seem to increasingly determine our fate.

JANUARY 17, 2020

When I was a hospital chaplain, the same situation would often repeat itself, maybe for just a few hours. Here it is the same. It's mysterious. A few weeks ago, our houses received a number of people who had fallen and injured themselves after scaling the border wall. Lately, it's been pregnant women. Today, we welcome three women, all expecting.

JANUARY 18, 2020

I've been wanting to visit one of the state-run shelters in Juárez. Today, I am going to go with Tina and Kathy to visit the school which is now in a clean, spacious shelter run by the Anglican Church of Mexico. It's a long half-hour car ride from the bridge. Tina and Kathy have been working there since the street camps were broken up.

I'd been wanting to spend some time with Tina. I am interested in her experience on the streets in a major U.S. city and here in Juárez. Before we get a ride to the shelter, she shows me the building where people apply for asylum and get into the process.

Tina runs into a lot of people she knows from the streets, the shops, and the school. She's a very expressive individual, and it is fascinating to watch her engage with people I might walk past without noticing.

We take an Uber. Our driver is a former police officer and father of a five-year-old. He scoffs at the idea that Juárez is more dangerous than any major city in the U.S. We drive southeast through the industrial part of the city. Juárez is much bigger than El Paso with more than twice the population. I see an industrialized part of the city I'd not seen before.

After greetings and introductions, Tina sets up a table for an art project for the children to create together. Just before dark, we help set up goals outside for soccer. Our driver on the return tells us about a new Uber service—female drivers serving female passengers. We walk back over the bridge with no delays. Sometimes the bridge is so crowded it can take more than two hours to cross. I ask Tina if there is enough shelter space for people in Juárez. She thinks there is. Some people do not feel safe in shelters and prefer to live on the streets.

Tina and Kathy are examples of the many people who do their work quietly here, adjusting to shifting conditions and needs. Maybe this is what people have always done in the community. You see something that needs attending to. You feel moved to get involved. You roll up your sleeves and get on with it. I like feeling part of it.

At dinner, a chaperone for a BAE group from a high school in Delaware says they were told by an immigration judge in New Mexico that there are now a million people in the system.

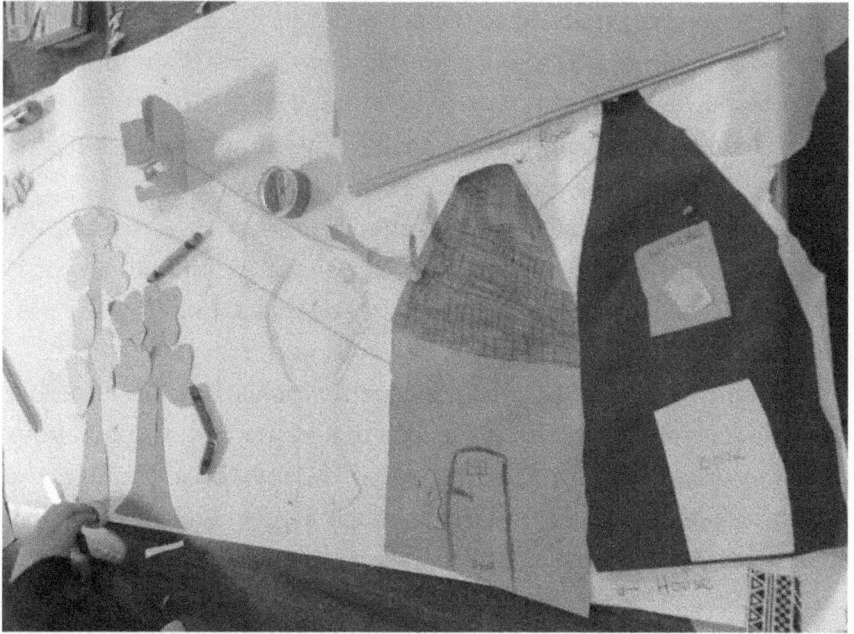

The children do an art project together.

JANUARY 19, 2020

The knock at the front door early this morning is so soft, it's hard to tell if someone is there. I open the door and look around. At first, I don't see anyone. Then I see a young woman looking through the gate in front of the parking area.

She is pulling a small caddy and asks whether we can help with an "emergency donation" of warm clothing. Temperatures still drop quite a bit at night. Her hands are icy as we introduce ourselves.

"Most places are closed on Sunday. I thought you were probably closed too."

Our house wears no identification but a street number, so I'm not sure how she found us. I have a good feeling and invite her in. A few guests and volunteers are having breakfast. We head downstairs to the clothes closet. We have one long winter coat left, and it fits. She takes a pink knitted hat, a new sweatshirt, some socks, and undies.

Then she shares a bit of her story. She is from a neighboring state. She has finally summoned the courage to leave an abusive husband. She wants to make a new start and likes El Paso. The Salvation Army is helping, giving her a case manager who will look for housing. I tuck her things into a cute tote, and we go back upstairs. This is someone who is going to make it, I say to myself.

"Are you hungry?"

She sits down, drinks some orange juice, and takes a banana and an apple for later. Several of my colleagues introduce themselves. We suggest she look into staying at one of the shelters for women without kids. After that, all I have to do is listen as she pours out her heart: her dreams, her doubts, the things she is learning about herself. I feel her courage, strength, and resourcefulness, and I tell her as much. After a blessing at the door, she is on her way.

I am so moved to be part of this community of care. We help people meet their material needs. More than that, we help people meet their human needs for dignity, respect, and belonging. We don't get bogged down with too many forms (though we have some), too many rules (though we have some), and layers of bureaucracy. We simply treat others as we would wish to be treated, as if we all have a stake in this human project. All of this is only possible with the generosity of the local community and a much larger circle of friends.

JANUARY 20, 2020

Finally, I'm on the insurance policy for the house car. This is going to make my life a lot easier. The timing is good because Chris is moving on at the end of the month.

Keeping the children up to date with vaccinations has been a thing. We love Immunize El Paso. They make sure vulnerable populations get their required vaccines throughout the borderland. But sometimes they run out of vaccines. The three families who went there on Saturday will all have to go back again.

In other news, our three-year-old seems to have taught the ten-month-old to scream.

JANUARY 21, 2020

This afternoon we have an all-volunteer gathering at one of the other houses. Every few weeks, we take some time for reflection, do some business, and recognize long-term volunteers who are ending their service. One of them is my colleague, Chris. I will miss him.

It is interesting to hear stories from the other houses. They deal with so many more people, so they have other perspectives. We are relieved to hear that Casa Vides will soon have another experienced volunteer. Caroline will arrive on February 1st. We also got approval to replace two ancient water-guzzling toilets, something I'd been advocating for.

We begin collecting data on guests who come with injuries, especially falls from the border wall. Hopefully, there will be some media coverage as a result.

After enjoying a meal together, one of my colleagues and I decide to walk home on this crisp night with temperatures in the forties. I feel both stuffed and happy.

JANUARY 23, 2020

An Indigenous man from Guatemala comes to one of our other houses for a short stay after being released from detention. He doesn't speak Spanish, causing difficulties in communicating while he was held. (There are twenty-five languages spoken in Guatemala.) His credible fear interview did not go well, and he was informed that he would be deported.

"Asylum Officers conduct a 'credible fear...interview' when a person who is subject to expedited removal expresses an intention to apply for asylum, expresses a fear of persecution or torture, or expresses a fear of return to his or her country."[2]

A few days later, someone hands him his immigration papers. He will now be able to take his case before an immigration judge. How this happened is a mystery.

WE ARE EXPECTING a mom from El Salvador and her six-year-old son with cerebral palsy. I happen to be on shift when two young and polite Border Patrol agents come to the door with our guests. This young mother, who could still be in her twenties, radiates serenity and devotion to her child who needs constant care. One of our guests offers to watch him and soon has him laughing while Mom is in the shower.

The journey these two made together from their home country must have been grueling. They leave for their twelve-hour bus ride in the evening. Her son will ride in her arms the entire way as he did on the journey here.

I SPEND QUITE a bit of the day at Las Americas Immigrant Advocacy Center where four of our guests are scheduled for a consultation. Las

Americas is one of two organizations in West Texas and New Mexico that offer free or low-cost legal services to people immigrating to the U.S. or seeking asylum. The place is packed, and there are many forms to fill out. One of our guests has difficulty reading and needs quite a bit of help.

I get into a conversation with a Catholic sister who used to work with the organization here. Now she does her work on immigration in Albuquerque. She talks about other challenges, ranging from fracking to uranium mining.

The executive director joins us for a few minutes. I ask her about the number of cases in the system. She confirms it is around a million. We've seen people paroled for several years with no court date. No wonder. Attorneys from Las Americas and the Diocesan Migration and Refugee Services (DMRS) have to carefully choose the cases they get involved with. You are very fortunate if you get any legal support.

JANUARY 24, 2020

We get word today that a beloved 26-year-old mother, artist, and activist, Isabel Cabanillas de la Torre, was assassinated in the early morning hours riding home on her bicycle in Ciudad Juárez. She was an outspoken advocate for women's rights and a member of the feminist collective Daughters of Maquila Worker Mothers.

Her fellow activists are organizing to demand an investigation and an end to the femicides and disappearances of women that have plagued Juárez since it became a center of cheap manufacturing for U.S.-based companies under the 1994 North American Free Trade Agreement (NAFTA). Women from rural areas often come to the city for these jobs and are particularly vulnerable.

JANUARY 25, 2020

Today I spend my day off in front of the Mexican Consulate, joining those calling for justice for Isabel Cabanillas and other missing and murdered women in Juárez. Femicides are not properly investigated in Mexico. Everyone knows it. I feel deeply troubled.

Protest at the Mexican consulate.

I see my friend, Zeb, for the first time since Standing Rock. He knew Isabel personally. From the consulate, we walk in procession to the *Sister Cities* mural. From there, a smaller group heads to the bridge to join the larger group of demonstrators coming from Juárez.

I'm emotionally spent and return home. Later I hear the two groups shut down the bridge for several hours, disrupting traffic.

I end my day with an evening walk to El Paso Street, lost in thought. It's the heart of a vibrant shopping district in the segundo barrio. Crossing the Paso del Norte bridge from Mexico at night, you are greeted by festive lights.

El Paso Street.

JANUARY 28, 2020

Hospitality given. Hospitality received.

Chris loans me his car for a few days of rest and relaxation. There is a gorgeous sunset and a new moon in the western sky as I leave El Paso yesterday. I spend the night in Las Cruces, New Mexico.

Dripping Springs.

This morning begins with a hike at Dripping Springs with views of the Organ Mountains. It is so good to be walking directly on the land.

Later, the drive to funky Truth or Consequences includes the usual checkpoint. Surveillance technology is proliferating around the world.

Deb at Dripping Springs.

JANUARY 29, 2020

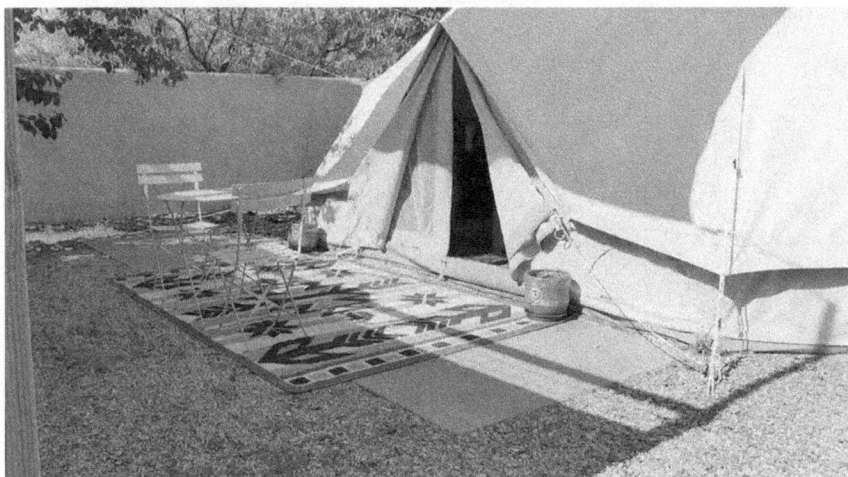

So this is glamping?

Staying in a glam tent and falling asleep to the night sounds seemed like a good idea when I made the reservation. This morning the temperature is twenty-seven degrees. Inside the tent, temperatures slowly dropped in the night, and it's now forty-seven degrees. I move to other accommodations. The natural hot springs relax and soothe my tight muscles.

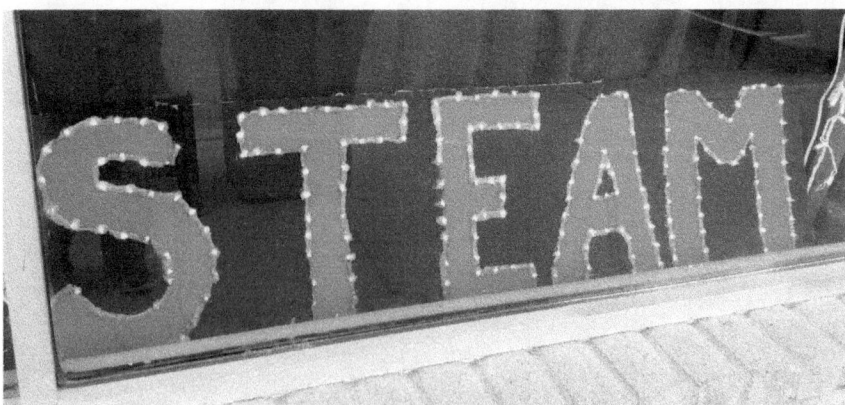

The hot springs at Truth or Consequences.

JANUARY 30, 2020

Pancho Villa's stash house is located next door to Casa Vides. It's being renovated as a restaurant and museum. During the Mexican Revolution, the place was raided by the U.S. Customs office. They found $30,000 worth of jewelry and a half million dollars in cash inside.

Pancho Villa's stash house.

Stash houses are very much a part of the current reality at the border and probably all over the U.S. These days, rather than being places to hide money and valuables, they are places where people are stashed by coyotes during segments of travel or dumped at the end of the journey. People are also stashed in these places by cartels and gangs for extortion or for human trafficking, either for sexual exploitation or forced labor.

A friend of one of our guests was last heard from calling from a stash house in another state en route to his final destination. Our guest has had no further word in days.

JANUARY 31, 2020

Driving home from the hospital late yesterday evening, I think it all got to me. I am spending the day mostly sleeping in my room with a stomach bug.

Yesterday afternoon we received a guest from Ecuador who had been released after a car crash just a few blocks from here. She was briefly treated for injuries. Her brother is still in the hospital. A friend of hers from Juárez was killed and another friend thrown from the car. The driver, probably a coyote, was uninjured and left the scene. My mind spins with questions.

Just before dinner, our guest says she wants to see her brother before making travel arrangements. It's been a long day. I got up at 4:30 a.m. in Truth or Consequences and began my shift at 7 a.m. I don't want to go, but there is no one else to drive. Carol, our new volunteer, and her sister offer to go along.

Once at the hospital, we learn the brother is still in custody and the staff can't give us the room number. I call a Border Patrol office to ask for help to advocate for a visit. The two agents decide that I can accompany our guest to the room for five minutes.

On the way home, our guest asks to stop at a pharmacy to get a phone card. Keeping in touch with family at home is a lifeline. We tell her one of us will help her in the morning.

FEBRUARY 2020

FEBRUARY 1, 2020

I'm still not able to eat. It may be more than food that I'm having a hard time digesting.

FEBRUARY 2, 2020

This morning, the family of five, one of two families living here when I arrived in November, set off by car for northern New England and their new home. Given the extortion and threats of violence they experienced, the odds seem high they will be granted asylum. I am happy for them and will also miss them. There are many adjustments they'll have to make. Climate, culture, the prohibition to work, and the need to learn English are only a few of them. I find the resilience of people from Latin America truly amazing. At the same time, I don't want to minimize the harm and the trauma of what they have experienced and the difficulties that lie ahead.

We hope our former BAE group's well-thought-out initiative will be successful. This family is their first sponsorship. It's a big commitment.

FEBRUARY 3, 2020

Happy 42nd birthday, Annunciation House!

This is the door to my room. Every room is dedicated to an individual who lived and worked among people who have little. I don't recognize many of the names.

The door to my room.

I am the only volunteer who sleeps on the ground floor. Our guests sleep in dorms or in smaller rooms on both floors. We all think it's important to have someone available at night downstairs.

This morning, I am still feeling under the weather when a Border Patrol agent rings the doorbell. I am the only volunteer in the house. He says he is dropping off someone who was injured in a car accident. I had no idea we were expecting anyone. I am feeling weak and want to be back in bed. I ask several times whether our director had authorized this.

The cobwebs begin to part. It must be the brother of the guest who had been in the car crash. When the officer opens the back door to the vehicle, I recognize him immediately. He is in a lot of pain and wearing only hospital scrubs on a chilly day. The officer has no wheelchair, crutches, or walker in the vehicle. Our new guest has no discharge papers explaining the nature and extent of the injuries with instructions for his care. He does show me several bottles of medications along with his immigration papers.

One of our long-term guests and I hurry downstairs and drag up a wheelchair. We need to be prepared for just about anything. Later we learn that our new guest spent two days in detention after being released from hospital.

My mind began to sort through the accessibility challenges of our house. Where can he stay? The step down to the men's dorm won't work. I wheel him through the mostly unoccupied women's dorm so he can use the facilities. He shuffles off on crutches with great difficulty, dragging one leg.

When I come back to check on him, his sister is settling him into the lower bunk next to hers. The women's dorm is the best available option. Sitting on the bed, he begins to shiver violently. We wrap a blanket around him. The other volunteers return. One of them brings up some soft, warm clothing from the basement. Our new guest says his pain level is a nine out of ten. He accepts water and soup, but wants nothing more substantial. Then he falls asleep. The tension in my shoulders begins to ease.

After speaking with our director, I leave a message for Danny, who arrives just before dinner. He wasn't able to reach anyone at the hospital for instructions before shift change. He does an exam and makes some practical suggestions.

FEBRUARY 4, 2020

The sister of the guest who arrived yesterday leaves this morning to travel to her family out east. After lunch, the brother is moved to another shelter where there is a nurse practitioner. Another ride does not help with the pain.

FEBRUARY 5, 2020

A dusting of snow fell in the night. Our guests and their children are overjoyed to see snow for the first time! In just a few hours, it's all gone.

FEBRUARY 6, 2020

It's exciting to get a tour of Casa Carmelita, with my colleagues.

Supplies housed at Casa Carmelita.

Zeb and other local grass-roots leaders founded this emerging community center which is already being used to stage supplies that will go to Juárez and to house a single-parent family.

Casa Carmelita is named in honor of Carmelita Torres, known as the Rose Parks of Mexico—more about her later.

FEBRUARY 7, 2020

We volunteers watch a documentary called *Harvest of Empire: The Untold Story of Latinos in America* (2012) together in the evening in our little hangout room. U.S. involvement in places like Cuba, El Salvador, Guatemala, Mexico, Puerto Rico, and more is the focus of the film. It's sobering. I was not taught these things in school. But it doesn't end there.

Around a million people of Mexican ethnicity were loaded onto trains to Mexico during the depression when work was scarce. It's estimated that 60% of these people were U.S. citizens.

"There's been a pattern now for the last one hundred years of Mexicans being recruited into the country, then shipped back out, recruited into the country, shipped back out of the country. The reality is that it's two countries but one economy. The Mexicans function as a reserve labor force in good times in America and as an expendable labor force in the bad times."[1]

The film concluded that "we are a nation of immigrants." While it is surely true that most of us have ancestors who came to the U.S. by choice from other lands, hundreds of Indigenous tribal nations had already been living on land now claimed by the U.S., much of it ceded by native peoples to avoid forced relocation by treaties that were later broken. Many others were captured and trafficked from Africa to the Americas and the Caribbean for their labor and skills.

I used to think history was incredibly boring. The way it was taught in my day omitted a diversity of perspectives and focused on dry facts like dates, wars, and powerful men. It didn't explain how we got here and how unacknowledged and unintegrated history repeats itself. With different voices and fresh perspectives, I now find historical context essential.

FEBRUARY 9, 2020

It is pupusa Sunday again at Casa Vides. These Salvadoran delights are time consuming to prepare and sooooo delicious!

The cooking sets off the smoke detector a few times. It's a mild day, and we can open the doors to let in some refreshing air.

Later we welcome a young mom and her son from Brazil. She crossed with her parents and other family members who are being deported. Having never lived on her own, she decides to return to her family.

There's been a decline in the number of people released to us lately. It's giving us a breather to do some spring cleaning and maintenance on the house.

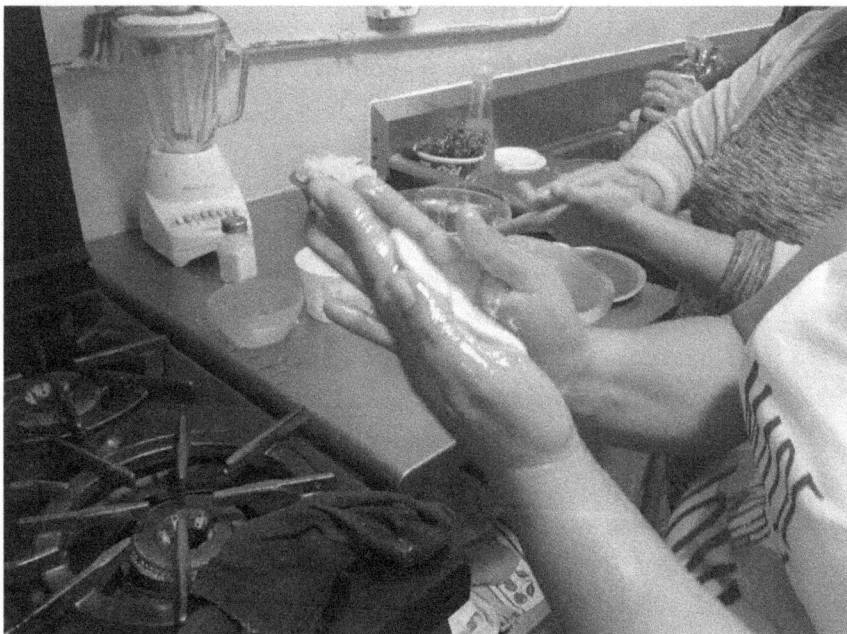

The morning starts with pupusas, a specialty of El Salvador. Oh, my!

FEBRUARY 10, 2020

The house remains strangely quiet. We take the opportunity to organize donations, complete some maintenance projects assisted by one of our guests who is very handy, and take care of some long-postponed errands.

We welcome a young woman from Cuba who will be reunited with her husband in Miami.

After lunch, some of the women stay at the table and compare notes on the work they have done: the long hours, the low pay, the working conditions in *maquilas*, the actual work itself. The tone of the conversation is matter-of-fact.

Maquilas or *maquiladoras* are factories that import and assemble components for export, duty-free. They employ mainly women and are known for poor working conditions, excessively long work weeks with no overtime compensation, and pollution. They offer multinational corporations in Asia and the U.S. a source of cheap labor and cheaper products for those of us who buy them.

One image has stayed with me: that of the *camote,* or sweet potato, which one of the women processed. I'm used to seeing an array of fresh produce from Mexico and other countries on display in grocery stores all winter. They are cash crops from the global south, often shipped thousands of miles to my table from places that have difficulty feeding their own people.

So many questions come up.

How do I benefit from inequities and exploitation? Why are some geographies so poor and others so wealthy? I could ask the same questions within a geography or country.

FEBRUARY 11, 2020

An outing from time to time lifts our spirits. Our volunteer team walks to Martha's for breakfast. It's my favorite place for huevos rancheros. The entire place is a tribute to the Dallas Cowboys.

I AM NOT on shift around 9:30 p.m. when we get word there is an issue at the nearby Greyhound bus station.

One of the people who was with us briefly will board her bus soon. She discovers she has two sets of immigration papers, her own and those of another guest. He's scheduled to fly to Miami tomorrow, but he can't board the plane without those papers.

After many phone calls, his relatives are notified. They'll be able to contact him. We're confident the papers will soon be retrieved.

FEBRUARY 12, 2020

I am always grateful when Border Patrol drops guests off in the morning. We welcome a very pregnant woman and her precocious two-year-old daughter to the house with plenty of time to get them both settled in before they travel on to their sponsor tomorrow.

According to Doctors Without Borders, more than ⅔ of people fleeing Guatemala, Honduras, and El Salvador left their home countries after a family member was murdered, disappeared, or kidnapped.[2] We hear difficult stories from many of our guests from all these countries: the murder of a parent, a brother, a cousin.

A few weeks ago, one of our guests got word that her son-in-law had been killed on the street. She collapsed on a chair in the backyard and wailed. I haven't seen that level of gut-wrenching grief pour out of someone since my days as a hospital chaplain. I sat with her, knee-to-knee, as her son and my colleagues formed a circle around her. It turned out that the victim wasn't her relative but someone he worked with. Sorrows accumulate in the body and need to be released.

Human Rights Watch reported that "the military coup d'état that ousted President Manuel Zelaya on June 28, 2009—and the attacks on journalists, human rights defenders, and political activists in the coup's aftermath—represent the most serious setbacks for human rights and the rule of law in Honduras since the height of political violence in the 1980s."[3]

The leader of the coup was a graduate of the School of the Americas.

FEBRUARY 13, 2020

There have been a lot of BAE groups coming through the house lately. In addition to the groups we host, groups organized by others often come for a tour of the house.

This evening a group of young men from a Catholic high school in Phoenix joins us for dinner. I sit next to a theology teacher who had been an Annunciation House volunteer in Juárez and Anapra some years ago. Now he's helping involve his students in remarkable service projects in many places in the Phoenix area. They are a more diverse bunch than I would have guessed.

He tells me about his one visit to Detroit. He'd been invited to speak about his experiences at the border at a university in midwinter. The cold definitely made an impression on him. He spoke about visiting a bookstore and coffee shop in the neighborhood and getting to know the person who ran it.

This could only be my friend Yusef's business, which closed when the building was sold. It's a small world.

FEBRUARY 14, 2020

Three women from Cuba will spend the night with us. At least one had been in detention for two and a half months. She is overjoyed that she can soon be reunited with her son.

We welcome a fourth woman from Cuba in the afternoon who fell from the border wall. Like others we've seen recently after their release from hospital, she has a back injury and arrives in a body brace.

If you wonder how it happens that people who live so close to Florida cross the border here, I would say it is a good question.

FEBRUARY 15, 2020

It's my day off today. Venturing out on my own into Juárez, I want to leave a flower at the mural by Isabel Cabanillas that seemed to foreshadow her death. It has become a memorial to her life. The mural is a self-portrait with blank spaces for eyes, brimming with tears. In the background are disembodied eyes. The words, *Te observan, or* "They are watching you" are painted at the top of the work.

Troubling mural by Isabel Cabanillas.

But I am just getting to know the city and I'm not quite sure where the mural is located. The neighborhood starts to feel sketchy, and I reluctantly turn around. I spend most of the day enjoying the vibrant area around the pedestrian mall, the market, and the cathedral. It is a gorgeous spring day and crowds of people are out enjoying it. I buy a finely beaded cuff from an Indigenous vendor and have my second meal of tostadas and lemonade at La Nueva Central.

The lively pedestrian street, Avenida 16 de Septiembre, named for Mexican Independence Day.

Walking back, the long line I'd seen at the bridge in the morning is gone. It's a quick walk back across to El Paso. Inside the building on the U.S. side, I see a Border Patrol agent speaking disrespectfully to a young man after the officer's dog had a thorough sniff.

I notice that some new technology has been installed. Not only is your photo taken, as usual, before you present your documents, but you also get to see it on a fairly large screen. A notice indicates that if you are a U.S. citizen, the photo will be deleted after your identity is verified. Otherwise, your photo goes into a permanent database. If you object, you are invited to request an alternate procedure. I consider objecting but feel tired of it all.

I see newspapers reporting thousands of women took to the streets yesterday in Mexico City. The presidential palace was splattered in "blood" after the gruesome murder of Ingrid Escamilla, age twenty-five, by her partner after an argument. The media published graphic photos of her body. People are outraged at the extreme violence, its exploitation, and the indifference of authorities.

ON THE U.S. SIDE, the river is called the Rio Grande. On the Mexican side it is known as the Rio Bravo. Between the sister cities, the river is held in place by a bed of cement to prevent it from meandering in the way that rivers naturally do. Now its path is rigidly fixed in place, inflexible. It's a bizarre and sad sight but avoids more border disputes.

Friends talk about swimming and playing on the riverbanks in their childhood. At that time these political boundaries were softer and more permeable. Today the entire scene is hardened and threatening.

The river lies on the south side of the border wall. You'd have to scale the wall to get to the river from the U.S. side, but the flow of people moves in the opposite direction. On the north side of the wall is an irrigation canal, part of a large network of canals in the desert southwest. Life-giving water is bled from the river upstream. The water is deeper in the canal than in the river, and we're told there is always a current. That makes it trickier to cross. Flood lights illuminate its concrete banks at night.

Four bridges connect Ciudad Juárez with El Paso. Two carry northbound vehicle traffic, and two southbound vehicles. Two of the bridges carry truck traffic.

FEBRUARY 17, 2020

Every day I get to see and hear evidence of the massive investments wealthy countries around the world continue to make to surveil and militarize their borders. The helicopters, in particular, get into my head sometimes. This month we learn that Black Hawk choppers are being reintroduced into the El Paso skies. I see one late in the afternoon, patrolling the river. There's no mistaking it as a war machine.

Sophisticated technologies are increasingly dehumanizing and invasive—cameras follow our physical movement, software monitors our online activity. There is the involuntary DNA testing, facial recognition, iris biometrics. This information is swept up into massive databases.

These infrastructures are flexible. They can target one group today and accommodate new targets tomorrow. Checkpoints can and do move around. I learn that the free movement of U.S. citizens was stopped for a time between the borders of California, Colorado, and Florida during the Great Depression.

Border Patrol personnel were deployed in New Orleans after Katrina struck in 2005. Border Patrol personnel were also deployed at Standing Rock just a few years ago.

———

I've been in El Paso for just over three months now, feeling at home in a shelter with people I've known only a short time. I notice most people refer to our guests as migrants, immigrants, or refugees. To me, it makes them sound like a separate species, not fully human, not like you and me. To me they are simply people in difficult circumstances. We speak different languages, come from different cultures, and have different histories. But we also share the common experiences of being alive—a shared humanity. We are the same, yet different.

I can relate to some of our guests more easily than others. We get frustrated with each other at times and need to have some straight talk or withdraw. But overall, there is peace and harmony in our little household. We work together to get meals on the table, get the kids off to school, keep the place in order, have some fun and quiet time.

———————

THE BABY who was a tiny infant when I arrived is three months old now and responds to us with smiles and eyes that notice his surroundings. Our twelve-year-old has become the leader of the pack of younger kids. He's taking on more responsibility for chores and seems more at ease. Our three-year-old continues to struggle with big feelings and seems to enjoy creating drama. We still can't understand most of what he says.

It may seem the lives of our guests are more uncertain than ours. But we get word that one of our community volunteers has developed a serious medical condition. She will be returning to the major city where she used to live for medical treatment and to be closer to family at least for a time.

FEBRUARY 18, 2020

I'll be focused on vaccinations again tomorrow morning. I thought I had the system figured out. But now there are discrepancies between what the schools are requiring and what the immunization clinic tracks. One of the kids has been kept out of school for the past few days by the school nurse.

Is this always so complicated? I can't begin to entertain the larger questions that come up around vaccines.

———

THERE IS AN ALL-VOLUNTEER training today at our place. Some of us will be doing work on the other side of the border when our new shelters open. We hear presentations on security from a Mexican police officer, a Catholic priest who serves in Anapra, and an attorney who shares a simple methodology to assess risk. We learn many practical tips. Are these cities more dangerous than many cities in the U.S.? Why are some groups at great risk? Journalists, priests, human rights workers, and activists, along with women and young people, are regularly targeted.

The different perspectives we hear are informative, thought-provoking, and disconcerting.

FEBRUARY 21, 2020

I'm finding that the best way to clear most of the guests out of the dining room after breakfast is to suggest practicing some English. Spanish and English speakers seem to have a natural reluctance to learn another language.

FEBRUARY 22, 2020

The situation at the U.S./Mexico border is always in flux. It appears that three programs, specifically, have been effective in reducing the volumes of people who stay on this side of the border while their cases go through a clogged system. These programs include MPP and two new fast-track programs being piloted in El Paso. MPP is now returning people from Brazil (in addition to residents from Central American countries) to Mexico. Around 17,000 people from Brazil were apprehended by Border Patrol between October 2018 and October 2019.

The two pilots are called: Humanitarian Asylum Review Process (HARP) and Prompt Asylum Claim Review (PACR). We're told asylum seekers can go through the entire process without leaving detention in as little as ten days. A lawsuit has been filed against the two pilot programs on the grounds that people do not have access to legal support and may be sent back in error, to face death or extreme violence.

We know that some people from Mexico, which is exempt in theory from MPP, have been told they have two options: to go to Guatemala or to voluntarily return home. Only when pressed, officials disclose a third option: seeing a judge. Meanwhile, specially trained Border Patrol personnel are being deployed to major cities.

What we are seeing appears to be part of a larger strategy by wealthy countries that's been going on for decades—not just in the U.S.—to adapt to climate destabilization by militarizing borders while ignoring the root causes of both mass migration and global heating. Industry trade shows encourage government agencies to invest lavishly in the latest technologies. This is a fast-moving train that is picking up steam. I've only been here for a few months, and my understanding is very limited. Reflection on my daily experiences here is how I learn and grow.

FEBRUARY 23, 2020

Greyhound, the largest bus company in the U.S., announces it will no longer allow Border Patrol agents to board buses to conduct routine immigration checks without a warrant. They will also not be allowed to enter areas of Greyhound terminals that are not open to the public. Customers who want to travel in peace are understandably disturbed by the practice.

There is a dragnet on major highways around border cities. Routine immigration checks have been and are conducted on buses not crossing or even approaching an international boundary. These checks are expected to continue under the new policy.

I HAVE a relaxing morning on shift. I finally remember to show some computer images of Michigan sand dunes to one of our guests who had no idea what dunes were. Children and their parents gather around to look at the photos and share some of their favorites from their home country.

FEBRUARY 24, 2020

This week marks the anniversary of the death of Juan Patricio Peraza Quijada in 2003 when he was a resident of the original A-house. At this week's all-volunteer meeting, our director brought a rendering of the neighborhood around A-house. No one could remember Ruben ever talking about what happened in so much detail. The picture he painted was so vivid—it was as though it had all happened yesterday.

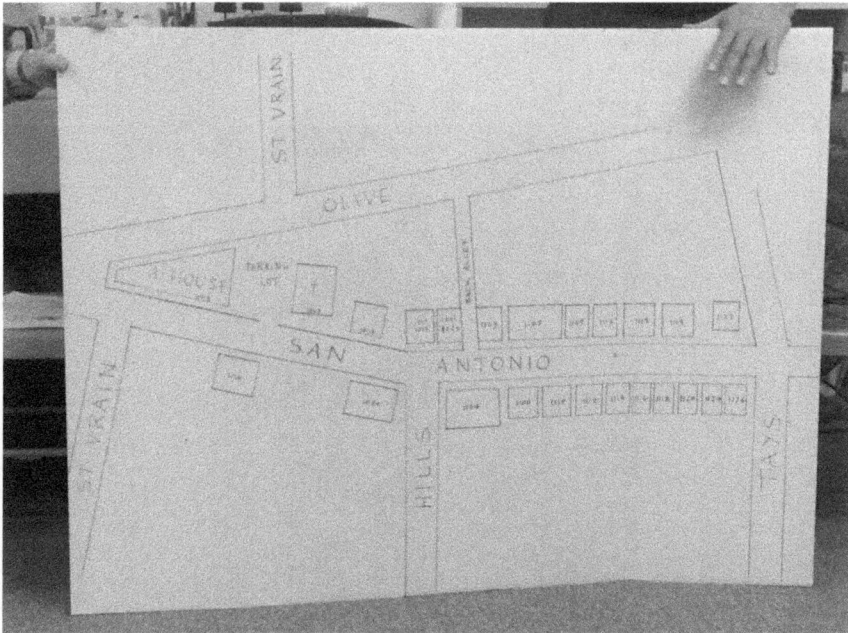

Site of shooting of an A-house guest near the shelter.

FEBRUARY 25, 2020

We are celebrating Caroline's milestone birthday with a visit to the El Paso Museum of Archeology, a little gem that includes the history of the Indigenous peoples of the desert. The themes of the photo exhibit by Las Cruces photographer, Wayne Suggs, are petroglyphs, land, and the Milky Way, blending the ancient with the cosmic.

The museum offers a wonderful view of the Castner Range, unscarred by towers and antennas and still deeply scarred in other ways. The gardens of the native plants of the Chihuahuan Desert are beginning to return to life. The beloved bright yellow poppies are scattered all around.

Poppies at the El Paso Museum of Archeology.

We opt out of continuing to the Border Patrol Museum just next door and have lunch at Cafe Mayapan. We tell our birthday girl that Neil Diamond will stop by this evening to sing "Sweet Caroline" for her.

FEBRUARY 26, 2020

It is instructive to notice what images and stories are lifted up in a community as most worthy of praise.

Lately, I've been struck by the special position given to "the conqueror." For example, the Conquistador Award is the highest honor in the city of El Paso. It recognizes those who have made significant contributions to the community in the past year.

At the Centennial Museum on the UTEP campus, a large painting called "The Conquistadors" is featured prominently near the entrance.

"The Conquistators" at the Centennial Museum.

The shields of the conquistador and the monk are on display at San Jacinto Plaza. When a wisdom tradition is co-opted and used as a tool of power and domination, it becomes a very different thing.

Conquistador plaque at the San Jacinto Plaza.

Plaque of a monk at the plaza.

FEBRUARY 27, 2020

One of the things I love about the work we do is building skills and confidence to take on a wide range of life situations.

Cata leads a baby birthing workshop.

It is a fun morning at the pregnancy and baby birthing workshop taught by Cata, our own nurse midwife. You just never know. One of our guests delivered her third child just fifteen minutes after arriving at the hospital.

FEBRUARY 28, 2020

In today's news is a ruling by the Ninth Circuit of the U.S. Court of Appeals, blocking the MPP. People seeking asylum often wait months to years for a court hearing while their application for protection is reviewed. These people are very vulnerable in border cities, easy targets for theft, kidnapping and torture, rape, and extortion. We know this from the stories our guests have shared.

It is said that MPP likely violates international treaties signed by the U.S. A government is not allowed, under these treaties, to send a person back to a country where they will likely be persecuted or tortured.

The expedited pilot programs, PACR and HARP, remain in effect.

WE RECEIVE three short-term guests from different countries just in time for dinner. One will catch a flight soon to be reunited with her mother. It was a six-month journey to the border for her, followed by two months in detention. Another says she has spent four months in detention. Two are wearing ankle monitors to ensure they appear for their court date.

FEBRUARY 29, 2020

Remain in Mexico protocols are back in effect.

After the ruling to stop the MPP was announced yesterday, the Paso del Norte Bridge closed around 7:30 p.m. yesterday evening and reopened this morning. An immigration attorney we know was on the scene when the policy was briefly put on hold. She tells us that Border Patrol agents were on the bridge in riot gear with the Mexican National Guard on the other side.

Later Friday night, the federal appeals court suspended its own order to halt the policy of returning asylum seekers to Mexico.

MARCH 2020

MARCH 2, 2020

My break has arrived, and I am on my way to Mexico City and Cuernavaca for the study program. I take the yellow Transborde bus to the Benito Juárez Airport. Having made a commitment to fly no more than once every five years, this will be my last flight for a while. I had considered taking a bus to Mexico City but traveling alone for a long distance through territory I'm not familiar with didn't seem like a good idea.

Colonization continues to show up in a new, corporate form. At the Juárez Airport, I see only familiar U.S. brands for food, drink, and car rental.

I meet our group of seventeen in Mexico City. Walking through the airport, I notice that some people are masked up.

We are welcomed by the Benedictine sisters who will host us for two nights. Their gracious home is just a few blocks away from the landmark Basilica of the Guadalupe.

As I take in the beautiful open courtyard, I notice large containers on every roof. I learn later that they store water to ensure availability when service is interrupted.

At the Juárez Airport.

Benedictine convent in Mexico City.

MARCH 3, 2020

Signs of Indigenous history near the Basilica of Our Lady of Guadalupe in Mexico City are few. The pyramids that once stood on the square are long gone.

The native people were suffering greatly in 1531, some ten years after the Spanish conquest, when four visions appeared to Cuauhtla-toatzin or Talking Eagle, who became known as Juan Diego after his conversion to Catholicism.

> *According to tradition, the Virgin appeared to a Nahua man named Juan Diego in December 1531 on Tepeyac Hill, north of Mexico City, where there was a shrine dedicated to the female Aztec earth deity Tonantzin. To this day, in Nahuatl-speaking communities (in other communities as well), the Virgin continues to be called 'Tonantzin,' and her appearance is commemorated on December 12 each year.*
>
> *Tonantzin means 'Our Sacred Mother' in the Nahuatl language, and she continues to be connected symbolically to fertility and the earth. It is not known precisely how the pre-Hispanic deity Tonantzin became connected to the Christian Virgin of Guadalupe, however, we can assume that many people of the time believed that her appearance represented a return of the Aztec mother deity. There are many myths surrounding the Virgin of Guadalupe, but she has been recognized by the Catholic church as a manifestation of the Virgin Mary. The Virgin of Guadalupe has become a national symbol of the Mexican nation, and she is viewed by many to be a special protector of Native American peoples.*
>
> *In conclusion, in the minds of many people living within and outside of Mexico, the Virgin of Guadalupe and the ancient Tonantzin are one and the same.*[1]
>
> —Professor Alan Sandstrom, Purdue University

MARCH 4, 2020

This morning, we board the bus and drive through beautiful forested hills to Cuernavaca. I unpack and settle into my casita at the Guadalupe Center. The grounds are filled with birdsong, a variety of trees, expanses of green grass, gardens, cacti, and flowers in bloom. Temperatures are mild. I am filled with joy to suddenly be surrounded by the abundance of spring after the austerity of a desert in winter.

The grounds of the Guadalupe Center.

The city's name comes from the Nahuatl word *Cuauhnāhuac,*

meaning "surrounded by or close to trees." It is, indeed, encircled by forested hills.

Many wealthy people from Mexico City now have weekend homes here. The local economy has been greatly affected by the sharp downturn in tourism, due to the violence that now permeates life throughout the country.

MARCH 5, 2020

I thoroughly enjoy Professor Antonio Ortega's presentation: "The Context of Mexican Culture Today." Most helpful for me was going deeper into the impact of the model of domination from the Spanish conquest and colonization from 1519-1521. Isn't power still largely understood as the power to dominate, exploit, and coerce' rather than the power to collaborate and co-create in service to life? We in the U.S. share a history of colonization and a familiarity with the violent tactics of empire.

We learn that the minimum wage of 123 pesos in Mexico (less than $7 a day) is the lowest on earth.

⸻

IN THE AFTERNOON, we walk around downtown and take a tour of the cathedral and market.

MARCH 6, 2020

Just a few blocks away from the trendy restaurants, shops, and markets we saw yesterday sits an abandoned train station. The federal government still owns the larger tract of land it sits on along with a neighborhood with paved roads and dusty paths. There people have made homes for themselves there without official permission. It is a place of material poverty.

Visiting with members of the community near the old train station.

We visit two homes to learn more about the struggles of the people. The sister who organized the journey tells us about the changes she has seen. People used to make shelters out of cardboard. Now they live in more solid dwellings.

Visiting with members of the community near the old train station.

Their situation remains precarious because they have no title to the land they live on and could be forced to move anytime. Their warmth, typical of Mexican culture, is like summer sunshine. Family is everything. These people may be living hand to mouth but are rich in spirit. It is both painful and inspiring to spend time with them.

As we leave the area and walk to the Children's Project, two police officers on motorcycles ride past us, their faces covered.

The Children's Project touches my heart more than anything I will experience on the journey. It's an initiative staffed by community volunteers. The building is simple. The needs are many. Their funding comes from a few nonprofits in the U.S. And now the requirements to access these funds are changing. The $20 per month that used to go directly to meeting the essential needs of each child is now going to the moms to start their own businesses. The people we speak with are not happy with the change. Whose voices get to determine what form of assistance is most useful?

Soila Luna who works with the Don Sergio Méndez Arceo Foundation spends an afternoon with us. We love her fiery passion and commitment. The foundation's focus is here in the State of Morelos. It works toward a more just, humane, and supportive society through training processes and the promotion of dignity for the most vulnerable.

Simply speaking, the truth is life-threatening. People doing work like this are a target group for assassination. What will help neutralize this brutality? I ask Soila for her thoughts. She feels strongly that their National Award for Human Rights is making a difference in its twentieth year. It is raising the profile of leaders making a difference who are often isolated in their work and unknown outside their immediate vicinity. With more visibility, she says, it is riskier to do harm to them. The visibility creates a sort of net of protection. This year they will not be offering the award. Instead, they will convene all the past award recipients for dialogue. This convocation will be held at the Guadalupe Center, where we are staying.

MARCH 7, 2020

The center recently built a wall between the street and the grounds. In the past, five guard dogs lived on the premises. The wall did make me feel enclosed and protected in contrast with my physical response to the border wall.

It is a wall-building time. Since World War II, the number of walls and fences between countries has risen from seven to seventy-seven. They seem to arise under certain conditions and come down when conditions shift.

Wall at the Guadalupe Center.

MARCH 8, 2020

Today we focused on Indigenous teachings. We visit the rural home of Ignacio Torres, a Nahual community leader in the mostly Indigenous *pueblo* or village of Amatlán. The Nahual are the largest Indigenous group in Mexico. Lisanne, his Canadian partner, was his translator.

Nacho, as he likes to be called, speaks of the cosmology of his people and the great cycles of deep time and the people's responsibility to live in harmony within the larger circle of being.

At home with Nacho (Ignacio Torres) and Lisanne.

The time of darkness ended around 2012, he said, and we are beginning to move back into a time of light. It's not a matter of seeing darkness as negative or light as the good. They are cycles to be accepted as part of life.

He describes how his community engages people who move

from the city to Amatlán, buy land, and build big houses. "We invite them to be part of the community. That means taking on responsibilities. Those who don't become part of the life here don't stay very long," he says.

It's difficult to do justice to the quality and nuance of the talk. For many in our group, this was the most powerful time of the journey.

Many Indigenous peoples of Mexico hold both an Earth-based understanding of how life is to be lived together with a great respect and reverence for the embodied teachings of Yeshua of Nazareth and his mother, Miriam. It is difficult for me to imagine what the life of the peoples of Mexico was like before Spanish contact or that of my own people in Europe.

Evidently in Europe, it took hundreds of years to destroy Indigenous cultures during the Dark Ages. As a result, the deep connection with place along with celebration of the seasons and the cycles of the agricultural year were weakened. Capitalism was replacing feudalism. The enclosure of the commons made the subsistence practices of hunting, fishing, and gathering that allowed people to meet their basic needs most difficult, fostered dependency and created the need to sell one's labor to survive. People began to leave the land and move to cities.

Indigenous peoples understand water, soil, air, and fire as sacred. The new economic system began to exploit these sources of life for profit. They were no longer seen as living elements worth of respect and care, but stuff. The witch hunts robbed women of their power as midwives, herbalists, healers, wise elders, business and crafts women, and more. It reduced their role to reproduction and devalued their labor.

We are only beginning to understand the effects of the collective historical trauma we have inherited from war, plague, extreme punishments, natural disaster, and expulsion. I wonder how the mass displacement of people we are seeing in the borderlands and beyond will affect our collective sense of self and our relationships with each other and the land.

I feel that Indigenous wisdom is the critical wisdom for our times. Seeing ourselves grounded in a place as an integral part of the greater circle of life—not as separate beings entitled to dominate and exploit—would be a transformative shift of perspective. We all have Indigenous roots from somewhere. My Indigenous heritage was uprooted from the soils of the north and the west of Europe. Almost nothing from the cultures of my ancestors was passed down to me. Yet I didn't feel this absence until later in life.

MARCH 9, 2020

Gabriela Hernández manages a shelter in Mexico City and talks about migration routes through Mexico. A river of humanity is always heading north. I am invited to share my own experience in El Paso with our group after lunch. Stories bring life and texture to the subject. They help people understand who is leaving their home and why.

MARCH 10, 2020

Signs of growing militarism and surveillance at home and abroad take many forms. On the way to the Women's Cooperative on the outskirts of Cuernavaca, a small military convoy passes us.

One vehicle carries a machine gun with an operator who looks poised to open fire. On others, soldiers stand with assault weapons at the ready. I'd like to say I'm not used to such public displays of force, but maybe the borderlands aren't so different.

Soldiers and their guns in a military transport vehicle.

I can't remember a warmer, more joyful welcome than the one we receive at the co-op. The women and a few of their children are there to greet us as we step out of the van. After they make us comfortable in their space, they sing a song of empowerment with a bit of humor thrown in.

The Women's Cooperative in the outskirts of Cuernavaca.

It's clear this group has been together for a long time and know each other well. They tell us about their lives before the co-op and the reluctance of their husbands to have them participate. There was one divorce over it, but the other men gradually came around. Now some are quite supportive.

The women earn a living from the sale of traditional crafts which locals are no longer interested in. One woman has gotten into physical therapy and sells herbal medicines. The drop-in visitors from the U.S. have also made a difference in their lives and income.

The sisters from the Guadalupe Center actively nurtured this group in the beginning. Now the initiative is mature. The women continue to come to the center for an annual retreat. I love meeting everyone and hearing about how they have grown as a community over time.

MARCH 11, 2020

It is a rest day. Most of my companions are in town strolling around and looking for gifts. I opt for a quiet day outside, drinking in the sunshine and appreciating the greenery, the flowers, and the chirping all around me.

Working in the compost.

Over the ten days in Cuernavaca, the fruits of the quiet, patient work of the nine sisters on the land and in the community become more apparent. It can take a long time to see a project do its work. Much of it is about shifting the culture. Cultural transformation is a long path and requires a commitment to stay the course. At the center, the tenderness and care for the grounds, the buildings, and the preparation of our meals becomes more palpable.

I regret not getting a photo of Laetitia tapping on the dried coffee cherries with a rock to release the beans. She comes from a coffee-growing family in a mountainous region of Mexico. She shows me how to pick the cherries without damaging the stem. I feel her deep love for the plant and the entire process.

Harvesting nopal or prickly pear.

Joachina tells me she had high cholesterol when she arrived at the center. Eating nopal, or prickly pear cactus, helps keep it within a normal range. I also miss taking a photo of Reyna, our pilgrimage leader, mopping the tiles of the main building. Carolina is younger and so much fun. She loves to sing and play the guitar.

Why didn't I exchange more money? I offer the sisters the rest of my cash to help the Children's Project buy a computer or support one of the other initiatives they mentioned. It isn't much—an act of solidarity as much as anything.

I'm grateful to have had the opportunity to pair this experience with my time in El Paso. It was all so informative and inspiring, warm and rich with relationships. The hospitality, humanity, and service to the community surely show a way forward.

Hanging the laundry.

MARCH 12, 2020

When I walk through the door at Casa Vides, I am surprised to be welcomed home with a round of applause. Everyone is having dinner. The latest BAE group from Boston made pizza on their last night at the border.

MARCH 14, 2020

The U.S. Supreme Court ruled earlier this week to allow MPP to remain in effect. The number of people coming to our homes has not gone up after dropping dramatically. No one is sure exactly why.

A few weeks ago, local leaders, including our director, had a tour of a new processing center here in El Paso. It will be able to accommodate 1,000 people with an area for unaccompanied young people. They say they expect people to be there for only a few days. Once the place opens, it will be difficult to know what goes on there. The existing detention center has a chaplain, and some clergy are allowed to offer services. So we have some sense of whether that facility is full.

And now there is the Covid-19 pandemic to prepare for.

MARCH 14, 2020

The two families who have been with us for a few months leave in the evening. I have vivid memories of the night they knocked on our door, wet and shivering after crossing the river and canal with temperatures near freezing. Rosaleen and I became closer after tending to them together.

The two young people have done well in school, and that has given them some stability. The women have had a different experience. They are impatient to work and get on with their lives. Uncertainty and anxiety have weighed heavily. Men are more easily able to find work that is more physical. It gives purpose to their days and money to spend.

The daughter of one of these women is still living in Honduras and has been under pressure to give money to a gang or cartel. Mom is desperate to earn money so she can help. Cartels are said to be better armed than authorities. They have also corrupted public officials.

Before leaving the house, we stand in a circle and pray for a safe journey. Despite the coronavirus, there is no question of not hugging. There are tears. The moms who met on the journey north look their best. My sense is they will be part of one another's lives forever. Eduardo asks me to return his school computer and some library books.

Rosaleen, one of our guests, and I walk beside them to the bus station, pulling their suitcases as a last gesture of friendship. I feel waves of emotion, preparing to say goodbye. An attendant at the bus station is particularly kind. Soon their bus will take them into the night.

MARCH 16, 2020

A search by what appears to be army helicopters is underway this morning over our home. The windows rattle every time they circle low. It goes on and on. I remind myself that border cities and the desert are also corridors for drugs coming north and arms going south.

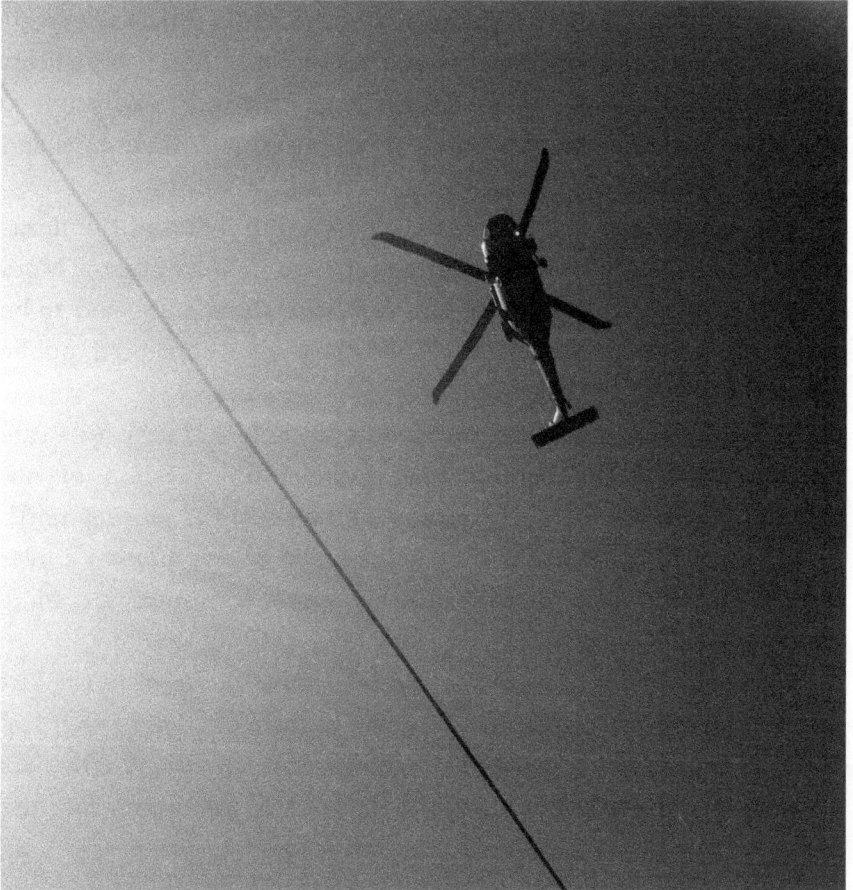

Army helicopters over our home.

MARCH 17, 2020

Brinkley, one of the young volunteers, is now living with us as house coordinator. We have begun taking and logging our temperature daily. I've been running a slight fever.

Ruben has been visiting the house daily to meet with the volunteers to see how our thinking is evolving. "What are your plans?"

We have elders in their seventies and eighties in the house, and they are at high risk. He is concerned and wants to know if we are taking the situation seriously. Every day feels like we're entering new territory as the realities of the unfolding pandemic begin to settle in.

Today I come down with the sniffles and am asked to isolate in a hotel for two nights as a precaution. Before I leave, Bea asks me how I really feel. I tell her it feels like a head cold, nothing more.

From the hotel, I am asked to move into the apartment at the back of the organization's administrative house. Brinkley gives me a ride from the hotel and brings over some of my things. I am alone in the apartment. It's not how I imagined spending my last days in El Paso.

Plans to deal with the virus are taking shape. Volunteers who are Covid-positive will isolate in this apartment. CDR will only take Covid-positive guests. The Mexican people coming to fulfill the social security death benefit requirement have moved from Casa Oscar Romero back to Casa Vides. Several of them are leaving soon. The Social Security office has closed. Oscar Romero will serve as the main site for any other guests. One of our young volunteers decided to return home and is leaving today. Another left last week. Yet another may be leaving soon. Rosaleen has reluctantly moved in with others from her community. Caroline has returned home. Bea, Brinkley, and Carol will stay at Casa Vides for now.

Businesses are beginning to shut down. I go for walks in the evening. There is almost no traffic. Spring winds blow dust and litter through the deserted streets. It all feels sad and strange. Still, there are only a handful of cases so far.

MARCH 19, 2020

I am still coughing, but that's normal for me with a cold. I'm not running a fever anymore. Ruben checks on me regularly. We'll give it a few more days and reassess. I have my things to pack up before heading to San Antonio next Thursday.

MARCH 20, 2020

The Centers for Disease Control (CDC) invoke Title 42,[2] a section of the Public Health Safety Act. Title 42 is a clause in a public health law that allows the government to deny entry to people without due process during certain public health emergencies—like a Covid pandemic. All noncitizens are now prohibited from entering the United States. That means the shelter in Juárez won't open for now. There will be no new guests at Casa Vides. A small number of guests will stay at Casa Oscar Romero. Everyone coming into any of the houses for any reason will be screened before entering.

I'm grateful to be able to say goodbye to our last long-term family via Skype. Manuel is one fine human with kindness, generosity, carpentry, plumbing, and auto mechanics among his many qualities and skills. His daughter has to leave her bulky dolphin school project behind. Our pack of girls is now down to just one.

MARCH 23, 2020

I cancel my stopover in San Antonio. The city is almost entirely locked down. I'm asked to make a list of nonperishable foods we'll need for volunteers isolating in the apartment. I research how the apartment can be sanitized as volunteers leave. It does me good to take a daily walk to the square. Sometimes Aida, who works at the administrative house, joins me at lunchtime. The coffee shops are still open for takeout.

I discover this mural just a few blocks away. The figure's hair suggests the cockroaches on his shoulder and forearm. It makes me smile when not much else does.

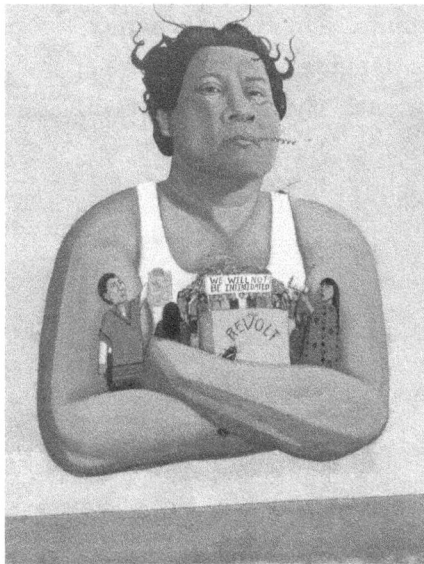

The mural that makes me smile when not much else does.

MARCH 29, 2020

I have been slowly settling into a peaceful solitude during these last few days in El Paso. Brinkley stops by from time to time and brings the rest of my things as it becomes clear that I won't be able to return to Casa Vides. And I also see Mary who lives in the apartment in the back of the house coming and going. I've been in isolation for two weeks, and the cold is long gone. This is my last day in El Paso.

MARCH 29, 2020

Today I am leaving for home. Brinkley picks me up and takes me to Casa Vides. Everyone comes outside, and we say our goodbyes on the sidewalk in front of the house. How dear these people have become. We've shared so much experience. Tears of sadness and gratitude well up. One of the families who was here when I arrived is still here. The baby has grown.

There are no hugs.

During my stay, I've regularly looked around at my colleagues and friends of the house and thought, we will never be together again like this.

Then Brinkley drops me off at the train station.

MURALS OF EL PASO

El Paso is a city of murals. It is a pleasure seeing my favorites as I move around the city. It's also fun to see new ones appear. Some beautify a dull space, while others tell a story of the history of the city. New themes emerge. Others are abandoned. Some murals are painted over with new ones. These are a few of my favorites.

Sister Cities, painted by Los Dos artists Ramon and Christian Cardenas, is on the corner of Father Rahm and El Paso Streets, close to the Paso Del Norte bridge. The intertwined braid of the twin sisters of El Paso and Juárez evoke the bond between the two cities.

The pair in this colorful mural called *Fronterizos* is by Jesus "Cimi" Alvarado. It is located on the wall of the El Paso Museum of Art facing Arts Festival Plaza and captures some of the cultural heritage of this place.

Chinche Al Agua, depicts a backbreaking childhood game, painted by Victor "Mask" Casas on the corner of Oregon and Father Rahm Streets. Some see these children as attempting to scale the border wall.

I'm always drawn to this mysterious mural. *Sagrado Corazon* by Martin Zubia, known as Blast, is located on Oregon Street across from the landmark Sacred Heart Church in the heart of the segundo barrio. What is the tree woman about to do with the flame in her hand? When you look closely, you see that the "halo" around her head are decals of coffins. Is this Tonantzin?

At the time it was painted, Indigenous themes were just beginning to appear in murals in the area.

Animo Sin Fronteras or Spirit Without Borders painted by David Herrera and El Mac, in a parking lot at Mills and Stanton Streets, has a poignant history. The son of the subject of the mural, Melchor Flores, was abducted by police in Nueva Leon, Mexico in 2009. The mural honors a father's determined efforts to get answers.

PURIFICATION
FEBRUARY–APRIL 2022

In the winter of 2020-2021, there were no vaccines. Everyone who was not doing essential work isolated at home and formed small "pods" to maintain social contact. I did not return to the borderlands that winter. The pandemic devastated my state, especially Detroit. A dear friend was hospitalized with pneumonia and tested positive for the virus. Mercifully, she was spared the typical symptoms and died peacefully. A dear cousin and her husband were hospitalized at the same time. He didn't make it. She was on oxygen for six months after her release from the hospital. She is now a Covid long-hauler. The virus has affected every part of her body.

The situation in El Paso was even worse. Our dear friend, Peter, tested positive for Covid and came to El Paso for treatment. It looked like he was going to recover, but he had a stroke after he was discharged from the hospital and into the care of loved ones. He died two weeks later. You don't have to know someone for a long time to have a special bond. Peter and Betty wanted me to return to Casa Tabor in Juárez for a weekend before I left for Michigan. But that last visit was not to be. There was no chance to even say goodbye. It was a cruel time.

The convention center, just a few blocks from Casa Vides, was turned into a field hospital. Eight mobile morgues were set up. It took months of waiting before the body of a loved one could be cremated. Peter's wish was to be buried in Mexico where he and Betty had lived and served for so many years. It was impossible to get authorization for that, so he was eventually cremated. His ashes are buried in Juárez among the people he loved. We gathered on Zoom for a funeral and later a memorial service.

Covid home tests were not yet widely available. Casa Vides, my first shelter assignment, became the safe house for the organization. No one was allowed in except for select volunteers and some new guests who had been in quarantine for two weeks. New guests with symptoms stayed at Casa de los Refugiados. Volunteers worked very long shifts there in Personal Protective Equipment.

My colleague, Chris, married a volunteer from CDR who was getting ready to start medical school. They had a small ceremony in Kansas where everyone wore masks except the couple and the officiant. I was grateful to be able to witness their union on Zoom. The internet became the glue that held many families and communities together. It allowed schools to hold classes during the worst of the pandemic in this country. Working parents struggled to juggle their responsibilities to their children, now at home, with the demands of their jobs. We adapted. It took a toll.

I got word that there was a tremendous shortage of masks in Latin America. A minister in West Allis, Wisconsin offered to collect extra masks for distribution to several countries. The Petoskey District Library agreed to be a collection point, and thanks to the generosity of the community, I was able to send in two large boxes of face masks and a small one that included face shields. Vaccines were in short supply around the world due to patent restrictions. It is a world where profit trumps life and protecting borders has become more important than protecting lives.

The virus was moving through the world in waves, so it was with some concern that I decided to return to El Paso in the winter of 2022 for another few months. The Omicron variant has been running rampant these last few months.

On the pilgrimage route, the second part of the journey begins after the anticipation, trepidation, excitement, and first tests of Initiation. Journeyers persevere as the physical demands of the route grow. They trudge across the plains, baking in the hot sun on long summer days. Transformation requires heat and intensity. The ongoing challenges of the Covid-19 pandemic and my assignment to a different shelter with many more guests, including those with significant medical needs, would offer plenty of opportunities for Purification.

Annunciation House or A-House, the organization's original shelter, is now my home. With its distinctive design, I think of it as El Paso's answer to New York City's Flatiron Building. During my first winter in El Paso, the building was closed for major renovations. By the time I arrive for my second visit, it's only been open for a few months. Everything is clean and fresh.

The renovated Annunciation House shelter with its distinctive design.

A-House is the only one of our three shelters that's wheelchair accessible. We can only accept people who can get around on their own, whether it's in a wheelchair, pushing a walker, or on crutches. We don't offer nursing care, but professionals do come in for home health visits. A team of community volunteers helps with transportation to pre-op appointments, surgeries, and physical therapy. The intensity reminds me of my days as a hospital chaplain. It's a good fit, though much more intense and demanding than my first winter in El Paso.

It's good to be back. I have a room on the second floor with a view of the mountain and the lone star of Texas, a landmark that is lit up at night. I keep my curtains open so I can wake up with the sun. On the ground floor, there's a sunny hangout room where volunteers can kick back and relax. On a full moon, I can go up to the roof where the panorama of the city is remarkable.

I have my first Covid home test upon arrival. So far, none of our guests at my house have gotten the virus during their stay, though a few volunteers have. I am now trained on how to administer the home test to others and how to log results into the state database.

Everyone is required to wear a face mask except at meals. New groups of guests who haven't yet been Covid-tested are usually tested outside in our small parking lot when they arrive. We volunteers are required to test ourselves once a week. We test our guests weekly at a Monday evening junta.

The city is using a hotel to isolate Covid-positive people. These people include not only those who have come across the border, but also people living on the streets. While the virus is still very much a reality, the crisis appears to be over, at least for now. The border remains closed.

Our circumstances have changed since my first winter. Our network now includes a growing number of congregations in El Paso and New Mexico. The notifications we receive every morning on the total number of people being released from authorities now tell us whether they've been tested for Covid.

Sometimes there are protected groups such as transgender individuals or unaccompanied young people who have been released as adults on their eighteenth birthday. There are also "spontaneous arrivals" such as people being discharged from local hospitals. Because of the intensity of caring for injured guests, we are the only house that sometimes receives no new guests for several days.

FEBRUARY 2022

FEBRUARY 16, 2022

I t is the birthday of a young guest who had been hit by a car. We sing "Happy Birthday" to him in Spanish. He's shy, but he seems pleased with his cake and card with goofy dogs. Our guest cannot read, so a volunteer reads him the message and each of our names. Later he has a video call with his wife. They have six children. He brings the card close to the phone so they can see.

As a result of the car accident, our guest's leg was amputated above the knee. He will be with us until the limb has healed, and he's been fitted with a prosthesis. He usually has appointments for wound care and physical therapy once a week.

FEBRUARY 19, 2022

It's my turn to take the overnight shift after covering the afternoon and evening. I will attempt to sleep in the office on a folding bed. Unlike the other houses, there's a volunteer on duty 24/7 here because of the injured guests.

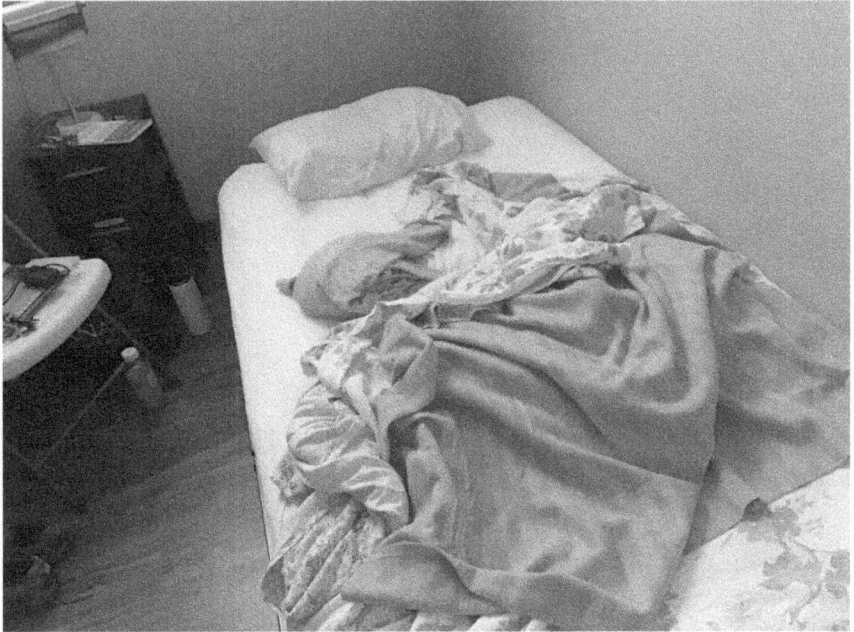

My turn for the overnight shift.

There is a welcome donation of winter coats for guests heading to the northern states. Transportation to pre-op appointments and surgeries needs to be arranged.

Dinner is at 6 p.m. I don't learn until 5:15 p.m. that the group that usually brings us dinner on Fridays isn't coming today. Two of our guests scramble to put food on the table. The kids like to watch a movie in the evenings, so the equipment needs to be brought to the common room and put away afterward.

One guest is released from the hospital in the evening after yesterday's surgery. She has new prescriptions. I find the discharge instructions less than clear. Rather miraculously, Miguel, one of the organization's board members who is a nurse practitioner, is in town for the weekend. He is here to see one of our other guests after spending all day visiting over a hundred people in our high-volume shelter. I could see the weariness in his eyes. He offers guidance that helps me prepare a new medication schedule.

I hand things off to the volunteer in charge of the morning shift who calls me a few hours later. Our new guest is looking for his immigration paperwork. I had misplaced it. It doesn't take long to find it in another guest's file, but what if I hadn't?

FEBRUARY 20, 2022

One of our long-term volunteers described yesterday as a perfect storm. I wouldn't go that far, but it was pretty intense.

We welcome eight new guests from many different places. That's a big change from last time I was here, when almost all of our guests were from Central or South America. Between us, we can communicate in English, Spanish, French, and rudimentary Portuguese. For other languages, we rely on Google Translate. It usually works quite well, except with less common languages. Some languages, including most Indigenous languages, are not available.

The new people arrive shortly before shift change when I was supposed to get a refresher on what needs to happen for new arrivals. We also have a short-term volunteer who will be with us for just a few weeks and needs to be briefed.

Three of the new arrivals have the means to stay at a modest hotel. They wouldn't be here for very long. After basic information is collected, we call the sponsor to ask them to make travel arrangements and share some important tips. As with my first winter at the border, guests who've been released by authorities have immigration papers that give them permission to travel, a court date in the jurisdiction of their sponsor, and possibly other instructions.

Two guests opt for an early morning flight. They are dropped off at the airport in the evening after getting a set of clothes, a shower, and a meal. One left this morning. Others are still making their arrangements.

I register someone from Cuba. He has some questions and asks to speak with a long-term volunteer whose Spanish is more fluent than mine. Everyone is supposed to work through the volunteer in charge first. This guest would not give up. He was repeatedly speaking to the fluent speaker who repeatedly pointed to me. (I'd do the same thing). Later, I took him and someone else down to the clothes closet. It is fun to watch them model for each other. Don't we all want to look good? You never know what people have gone through on their journey. I cut off the search at one point because there are others waiting. Off they go to shower.

The ropería *or clothes closet.*

At dinner, I formally welcome our new guests and repeat some of the basic rules of the house. I invite one of them to offer a prayer according to their tradition before the evening meal, which is our custom. I must say, this time I was very touched. Our guest spoke from the heart about his joy looking forward to being reunited with his wife who is already here in the U.S. He'll have his day in court, and we will not know what happens. He was one of the ones who left after dinner, motivated to spend the night in the airport to get an early morning flight to be with his partner as soon as possible.

The guests who've been here for a while recruit the new people to help clean up after dinner. The floors are mopped. The trash is taken out. Any leftovers are labeled, dated, and put in the fridge. Attendance is high for the evening movie. Then it's lights out at 10 p.m.

It's always a gift to have some quiet time in my room to wind down before sleep.

FEBRUARY 21, 2022

I wish I could show you their faces. The children bring me so much joy and delight. The energy of the house would be very different without them. The playroom is next door to my room. I love hearing their soft voices and laughter.

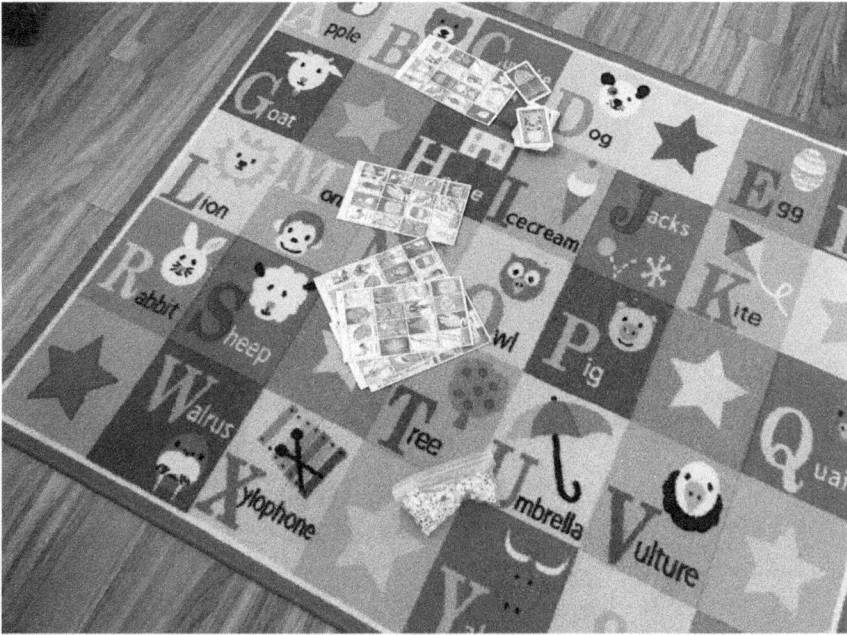

We have two families in addition to the single guests. One will be with us for a while. They have a little one around three years old, my favorite age, and a six-year-old who is in school (more kudos to the graciousness of the El Paso schools).

Another family has a nine-year-old and a thirteen-year-old who is a great help in preparing the dining room for meals. The younger one created the artwork I put up by the office when I am on shift. Mom came over the border wall and is recovering from surgery. They'll probably be leaving soon.

A family from Haiti with a three-year-old spent just one night a few days ago. Mom was seven months' pregnant. We offered them some diapers and baby food for the journey to their sponsor. Mom also asked for powdered formula to take to the airport. We just learned this morning that another brand had been recalled. One of the volunteers was combing the storage areas this morning to dispose of it. Always something...

FEBRUARY 22, 2022

A corner of the common area was briefly turned into a barber shop yesterday. Betty, one of the community volunteers, brings her clippers on Monday mornings. One of the guests who's had some experience as a barber works his magic and has people looking good. That's particularly nice for the three guests who are leaving this morning.

Betty and her clippers.

Our makeshift barber shop.

FEBRUARY 24, 2022

When I arrived in El Paso a week and a half ago, half of our adult guests were badly hurt. All but one had come over the wall and had leg injuries. We saw some of these people at Casa Vides in 2020, but the injuries we're seeing now are worse. First, the broken bones are held in position by an external fixator. After the second surgery that removes the fixator, guests get a boot and are ready to travel in just a few days. Sometimes there are broken ribs and back injuries.

One of our older guests has a doctor's appointment today. He has a complicated fracture just above the ankle. It may take three months to heal, and it's not clear whether he'll be able to walk again.

We keep an updated sheet of instructions for each individual, based on their doctor's orders. We bring pain and other prescribed medications to these guests three times a day. We leave 2 a.m. medications with them on our last round.

With so many injuries, it means there are fewer people to call on to help with chores, but that hasn't been a problem. People are eager to have things to do and usually take the initiative. The rhythm of the days and keeping things clean and in order creates structure. This helps temper the uncertainties of our lives and the chaos of these times.

At mealtime, it gives me a warm feeling to see everyone pitching in to put food and drink in front of those who can't serve themselves —and take their plates to the kitchen for them after they've finished.

I took a call this morning from the hospital we use most often. They are researching places where their patients can go after discharge because the numbers of incidents and injuries are increasing. That's a conversation for our director.

I understand that bearing witness to difficult things shifts them. But sometimes it's difficult to not look away.

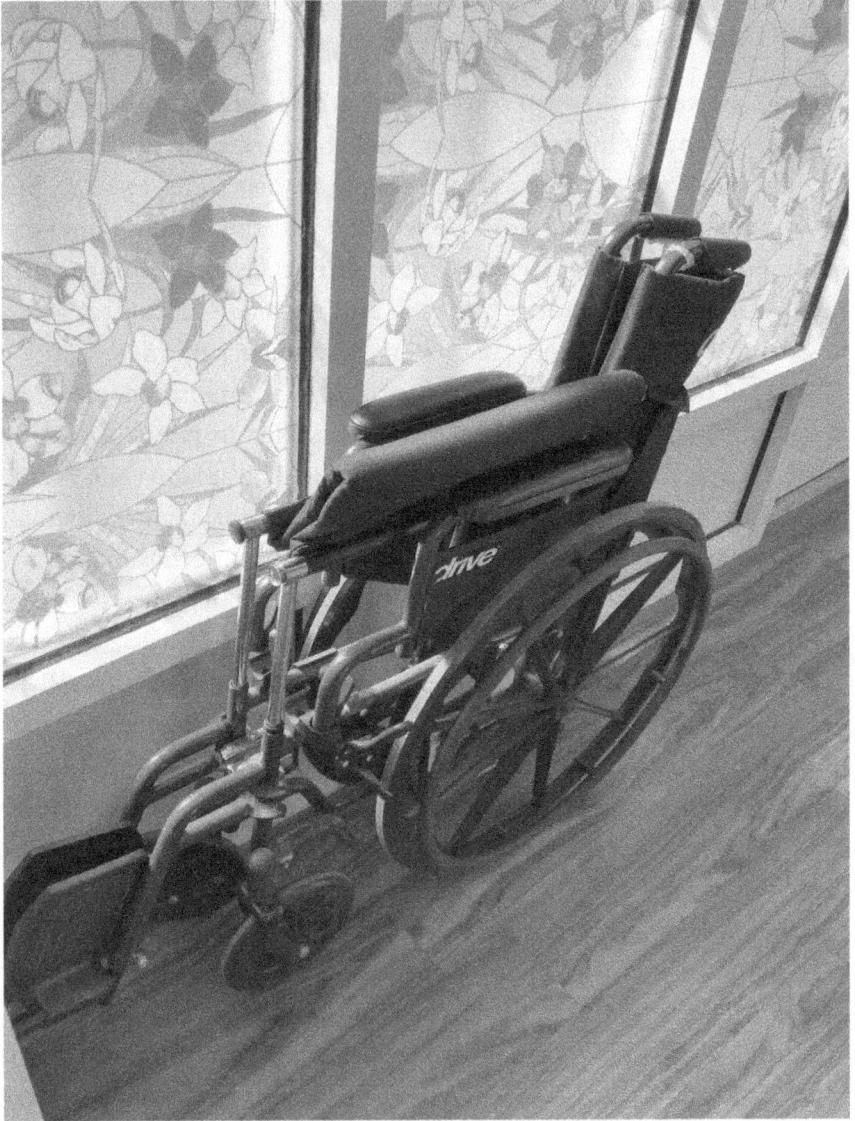

We always have a wheelchair at the ready.

FEBRUARY 25, 2022

You might remember the birthday cake and card that were offered to the young father of six children last week who had been in an accident. Sometimes initial details are fuzzy and not quite accurate.

He crossed alone somewhere. There was a chase, and he ran across Interstate 10 into oncoming traffic. He was hit by a vehicle. Evidently, authorities called for help and left him to his fate. That means he is not officially in the system with immigration papers and a court date. He will likely either find a way to return home to his family or begin a life here in the shadows.

FEBRUARY 26, 2022

I finally get to see this one. There were tears before smiles. I've missed her so much.

Deb and Bea.

Two years ago, it was Bea who waited at the El Paso train station for me for almost an hour while authorities held us up on the tracks and took seven people off the train. She and I spent a lot of time together when I was assigned to Casa Vides. She took me under her wing and made sure I was properly introduced to people in the community and included in the social life outside the shelter.

FEBRUARY 27, 2022

Lately, I've been involved with several conversations between two attorneys from Las Americas and two of our guests.

These two attorneys focus on the detention centers and not on asylum cases. They help get the most vulnerable people released, usually because of medical conditions. Our two guests had both been in detention for three months.

Sometimes these attorneys enlist law students to help complete an application for asylum, help find sponsors for the people they're supporting, apply for a donation for travel, and transport them to ICE check-ins.

There are so many people in the system. It can take months of sleuthing to find representation. Not everyone is successful in getting this kind of help, especially at the border.

FEBRUARY 28, 2022

I teased the girl yesterday evening, saying she couldn't leave until she finished the puzzle. She loves puzzles. Her brother proudly points to the finished product at breakfast this morning. The last piece went in just before bedtime, they said.

I'll miss these two young people. Mom has been healing after her surgery, so the family is leaving today. They'd been here since before I arrived. I'm both happy and sad to see them go. You can get attached.

The puzzle is so colorful, full of butterflies, dragonflies, and more.

A bright, beautiful puzzle.

MARCH 2022

MARCH 1, 2022

After enlightenment, the laundry...

There's a lot of it when families leave: sheets, towels, and blankets. And there are always tons of dish towels and dish cloths. It may not be the most glamorous task, but you get some quiet time away from the phones and other interruptions.

We wheel the load four blocks to the administrative house where there are clotheslines. Our guests have access to the two washing machines and dryers on site.

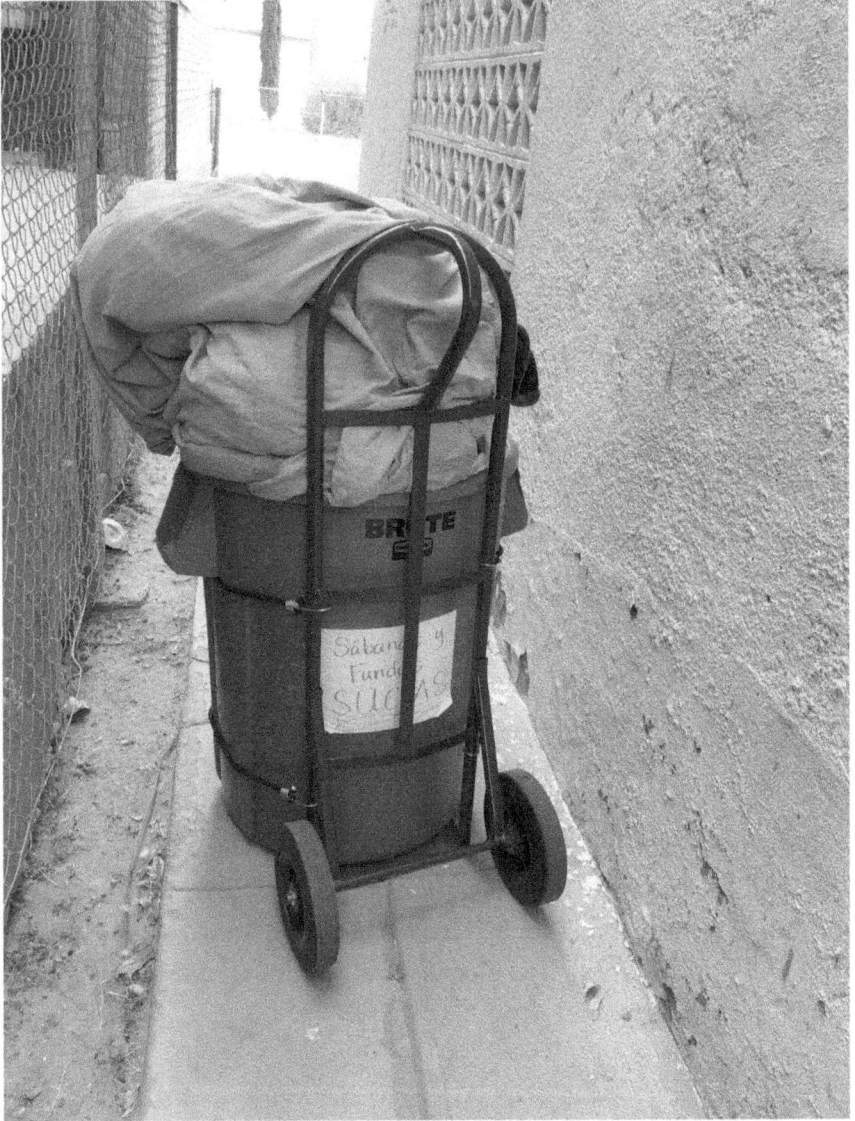

After enlightenment, the laundry...

MARCH 2, 2022

I was handed this little bundle when her parents helped with the cleanup after dinner. She was just four days old. I don't have children of my own or nieces and nephews, so I enjoy interacting with the infants and children...most of the time.

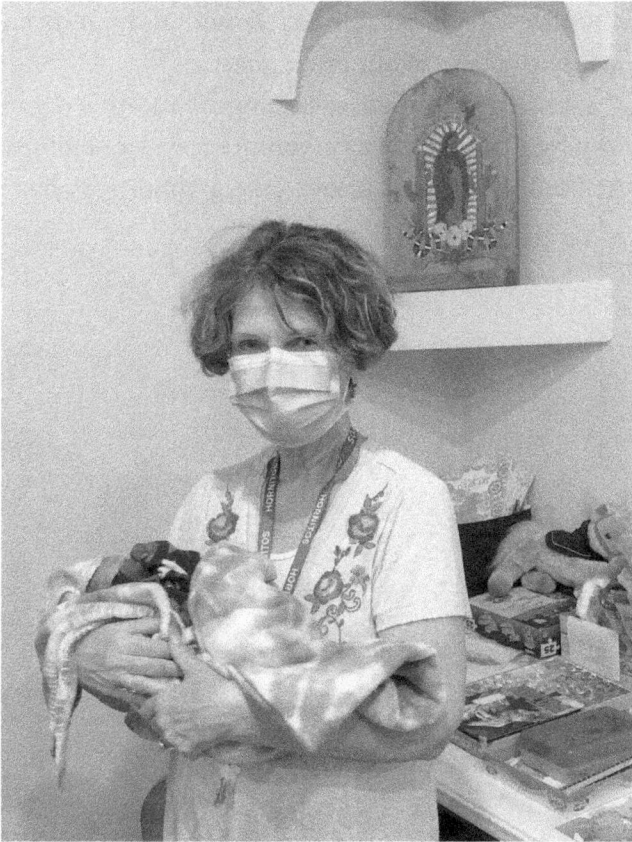

Deb holding a four-day-old infant.

MARCH 3, 2022

Groups of university students and adults from congregations used to come here regularly to see for themselves what goes on here. There hasn't been any of these groups for nearly two years since the pandemic began, so I'm happy to say the Border Awareness Experience groups are starting up again. The first group will share a meal with us on Friday. They'll be able to talk with our guests and stay at our big house with many of our other guests.

Giving a tour of the house, talking about the organization's history and why I came here as a volunteer was one of my favorite activities at Casa Vides. One of our young volunteers has taken on this role.

MARCH 4, 2022

I enjoy a laid-back and relaxing day off. I still don't know too many people outside of those who constellate around this work, so sometimes I spend the day alone. It's one way to release some of the intensity.

A new mural designed by an eleven-year-old.

I am seeing signs of spring here in the Chihuahuan desert. Wandering around the second barrio after my favorite breakfast of huevos rancheros at Martha's, I discover a new mural that is not quite finished. Not only that, but I meet the mother of its designer. Mom is up on a ladder filling in spots here and there while her daughter is in school. Her daughter was just eleven years old when she designed it, winning a city-wide contest with a theme of racial harmony. Mom is so proud and hopes the mural will inspire people to respect each other as members of one human family. The mural will be finished in a week and dedicated shortly after. It's one of a group of new murals on the same building.

MARCH 6, 2022

Jeff and Antony are two of the volunteers at our house. When I took this photo, they were absorbed in all the details involved in receiving another injured guest who came over the wall. Like most, she will need another surgery in a few weeks.

Jeff is a long-term volunteer, a former information technology professional and now a Unitarian Universalist minister. He speaks fluent Spanish, is detail-oriented, and very methodical. He's able to turn the complexities of hospital discharge papers into the sheet we'll use to bring our new guest the medications her doctor has prescribed. There are also doctor's appointments to be made and more. Jeff is always available when I have a question or need some help. Jeff's wife, Carol, was here last month to pitch in for a few weeks.

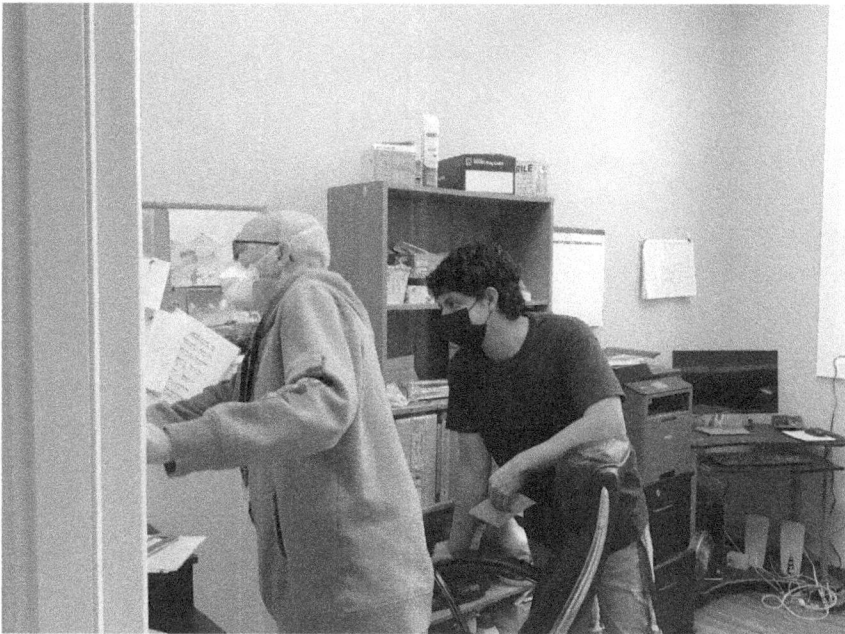

Jeff and Antony.

Antony will be with us for the month. Imagine. When he was fifteen years old, he and his family lived right here in this house for several years. He went to one of the local high schools. Now he's back as a volunteer to pay it forward. He brings a youthful spirit, a love of art, and an understanding of the culture of many of the people we serve. I appreciate his concern for the quality of life of our guests, especially the ones who are injured.

Adults can only watch so many kid movies with the young people. A few evenings ago, Antony proposed a game of *Lotería,* also known as Mexican bingo, with charming images in lieu of numbers. The game brings people who often stay in their rooms after dinner back to the table. Antony likes life in the U.S., but misses his grandmother, who lives in his Central American country of origin.

In this work, you get to bring all the capacities, skills, experiences, and interests with you. You never know what the day will bring and what you'll be asked to do.

MARCH 7, 2022

There are moments of overwhelm and exhaustion. Then there are moments of grace and beauty. It is a practice to be willing to move with whatever presents itself.

We went from a home where we knew everyone's name and people did their preferred chores to receiving twenty-six guests from one Central American country all at once. For the next few intense days, those on shift have constant demands on their time and attention.

The phone rings constantly with information from sponsors about bus tickets and flights. There is commotion everywhere as the new people try to find quieter spots to talk to relatives and friends. There are forms to be filled out, toothbrushes, linens, and towels to be delivered to beds, and drivers to be lined up for departing guests. Meals need to get on the table followed by cleanup. Everyone who is able pitches in.

Then, just as you think you have a moment to catch your breath, there is a round of medications to be delivered and people who need transportation to doctor's appointments or surgeries. There are people asking for cough syrup or something for the flu. I can't call people by their name anymore, because there are too many names to learn.

Mary, our laid-back and upbeat house coordinator, asks me to make an announcement before dinner that there will be a trip to a nearby park and soccer for those able to play. Almost everyone heads out in a conga line, including three guests in wheelchairs. I stay at home. Now there is time to breathe.

For the first time since the beginning of Covid, guests are free to come and go. This is huge for them. The other house rules are unchanged. We ask our guests to be in by 10 p.m. and not to use the house refrigerator for personal food and drink—it's a big enough job dealing with house leftovers. We also ask them not to bring food and drink to their rooms to avoid ants and other uninvited visitors.

I am on the combined p.m. and overnight shift, which is usually quiet. But not tonight. A message comes in around midnight to expect someone to arrive by foot from the bus station around 6:30 a.m. He has a court date and will need a Covid test. Then ICE calls around 1:30 a.m., asking to speak with someone. There is no one here by that name. The individual in question was not sending in their daily photo. Checking in with a daily photo that monitors your whereabouts is a gentler alternative to the ankle monitor worn by our guest with the court date. Often the phones people are given that are restricted to this function don't work. Uninterrupted sleep didn't come after all that.

Then in the morning, well-rested, I walk into the common room where a prayer before breakfast is in process. I feel bathed in tenderness and a sense of community. There are other new guests, including a young person around six years old. Everyone is talking, laughing, and enjoying the meal.

Clean-up is a big job.

Sometimes I ask myself what I am doing here. I tell myself that I no longer have the energy and stamina for the work. Then this morning, I think to myself, there is nowhere I'd rather be than here, in the middle of it all.

MARCH 9, 2022

It's good to get outside and take a walk. This is my new favorite coffee shop, which is also a bike shop, just three blocks away.

Podium Finish, my new favorite coffee shop.

MARCH 10, 2022

For the first time in a month, I find myself losing patience with one of our guests, one of the last to move on from the wave of people we welcomed last week.

"He hasn't done a thing to help out," says one of our long-term guests when I am on shift.

She is actually referring to two individuals who spend quite a bit of time out and about. We don't have so many able-bodied people in the house right now to help with chores. We all feel it, especially the one who's been doing most of the cooking. But other things needed my attention.

There are three people leaving for the airport at the same time, including this fellow. I need to interpret for our French-speaking guest and his attorney. We have another guest leaving for surgery in a half hour. Then I am interrupted by the guest I mentioned, insisting on attention.

He can't find the case and the cord for his new cell phone. He is pretty agitated. Cell phones are lifelines for our guests. I get that. But drama is unusual in our home, though the chaos and the real difficulties of their lives are always felt in the background.

After a fruitless search, he finally mentions a conversation with the volunteer who'd been on shift that night. It turns out Jeff knew exactly where the things were but didn't know who they belonged to. "Mischief managed," as he likes to put it.

When I take the guest back to the dorm to see if his sheets and towel have been put in the big hamper, I find a set wadded up on the next bunk.

"They're not mine," he said.

I take a deep breath. "Well, would you help me take them to the common room?"

He does.

I'm used to our guests and my fellow volunteers being eager to pitch in with all that needs to be attended to. I am annoyed, but that doesn't mean I get to act it out. It affects everyone around me.

Now I can smile and invite myself to own my reaction. How many times have I minimized the needs of others and insisted that my needs needed to be front and center? It's interesting how often these dramas are about stuff, money, and time—and whose needs come first.

MARCH 11, 2022

The morning sunlight is streaming into the common room. Everything is luminous and radiant. One of our injured elders sits in meditation with his face aglow. One of our young people is drawing quietly nearby. It is a sweet scene, just the two of them with me as the observer.

A bit later, I ask the older guest if he has any interest in having a go at an adult coloring book, another meditative experience. He nods.

The days pass.

Adult coloring books are calming and help pass the time.

MARCH 13, 2022

I was going to say that I prefer the a.m. shift (6 a.m. to 2 p.m.). I like the feeling of cool morning air on my face as I walk around the building to do a security check. The cool, clear light of Venus always greets me low in the eastern sky. And there are usually a few hours of grace to take care of basic tasks like making sure the bathrooms are stocked with toilet paper before the phone calls, appointments, departures, and arrivals begin. Today is an exception.

I get word that I will be receiving the guest we'd been expecting the day before, bright and early at 6:30 a.m. This individual had been turned away from her flight, apparently because she couldn't get out of her wheelchair and into her seat. She was also not able to communicate with airline personnel in either English or Spanish.

She'd come over the wall and fallen, sustaining injuries to her foot and spine. The medical transport person says she isn't ambulatory. What? We've been assured she is. It is a requirement for our house that guests be able to move around and tend to their basic needs.

She looks so young, weak, and tired. I offer her water and a blanket to wrap around herself. After that, I call her husband to let him know she is here and to get more background. I sort through the discharge instructions, create a sheet with the list of the medications and timings, and give her what has been prescribed. She is able to eat some breakfast. A guest helps her in the bathroom. I don't want to take any chances until our house coordinator arrives.

Later it seems that she can maneuver very slowly with a walker. She is able to lift the injured leg and hoist herself into bed. She's sleeping a lot. There is an incident afterwards involving a fall. I wasn't there and don't know the details.

Later I get several phone calls from her country's consulate, at her husband's request, with offers of practical assistance, including interpretation. She speaks the most common Indigenous language in her country. Our house coordinator will get a phone for her after her husband transfers the money. That and his assistance will help us communicate with her.

The phone rings a lot today. I receive two calls from medical organizations in the morning, asking about our capacities to serve injured people. Their sighs of disappointment register physically in my body. The people they need placements for are not ambulatory. I've received several other calls in the past month. The need seems to be growing.

Around 9 a.m., it begins to snow! Enormous flakes fill the sky, delighting the children and many of the adults.

Snowflakes fill the sky.

Shortly before my shift ends, a bus pulls up and the seventeen new guests we are expecting get off. Our two young volunteers are here and ready to help with everything that needs to be done.

What a day... I think it's been the most demanding since I arrived. Good thing I have the weekend off and will have some fun to look forward to with a friend who is coming to town.

MARCH 14, 2022

I enjoy a restful weekend off, exploring El Paso with my friend. Spring is in the air. Grasses are just beginning to turn from green to brown, and tender limey-lemony leaves are starting to unfurl.

We relax at the San Jacinto Plaza where there are photoshoots going on all around us—a wedding and many *quinceañera* celebrations.

San Jacinto Plaza is a popular spot for wedding and quinceañera *photography.*

MARCH 15, 2022

It's a day when I'm focused on the house laundry that piles up. I ask one of our guests for help with the door. He takes the big tub on wheels from me, and I hold the door open for him. I ask him if he wants to go for a short walk to Casa Teresa with me. He says he is leaving at 10 a.m. for his flight. He tears up and is quiet for a moment. Clearly deeply moved, he expresses his gratitude for the kindness offered at the house and gives me a hug. I don't know his name and guess he arrived with a group over the weekend while I was away. It doesn't matter that I don't know him. He needed to express what the hospitality had meant. We never know what the people who come through these doors have been through at home, during their journey, in detention, or coming over the wall.

I bring the clean sheets, towels, and things back to the house, unfolded. Helping fold the laundry gives the injured guests a way to contribute to the operation of the house.

The evening meal includes a BAE group who've just arrived. Over forty of us pack ourselves around the tables. After dinner, the group handles the cleanup, which gives our guests a break. Then they go up to the chapel for their end-of-day reflection.

The rest of us get together for our weekly house meeting. While we wait for the results of everyone's Covid tests, Jeff asks the guests what they learned from their conversations with the students. They have a lot to say. One injured individual who had come over the wall said it was important to her to be able to share her story—how she had fallen and lay on the ground for seven hours in an uninhabited desert area before she was found.

We talked about Title 42 at our volunteer meeting this morning. Some people see no alternative but to attempt to cross the border wall. I am realizing how important it is to question the stories we are told by the media. Immigration is a charged topic for candidates for public office to leverage during their campaigns and while in office.

Over the weekend, there was an official announcement that Title

42 would no longer be enforced for unaccompanied young people. If that were the case for adults, the volumes of people going through our houses could increase significantly. It might also mean that we would see fewer people coming over the wall and breaking their bodies. We have two people scheduled for surgery today. Another individual who also fell from the wall joined us a few days ago.

I have a lot of respect for the organization's ability to move with shifting circumstances. I couldn't do it!

MARCH 16, 2022

We welcome yet another woman who came over the wall and will need surgery this week.

The border wall.

After my shift, I encounter a sweet scene in our tiny parking area behind the building: sixteen new guests have arrived and are being tested for Covid in glorious eighty-one-degree temperatures. It is not a group of single men this time. The new people are all families with young children. The early evening bathes them and the two volunteers in soft light.

MARCH 17, 2022

The last individual from the latest wave of guests is leaving for Milwaukee today. He shows me a drawing and explains what it means to him, but it all goes by so fast. My Spanish continues to improve, but there are many accents from many places—and different regional and individual speech patterns. Our guests come from places as far away as Angola, China, Congo, Nigeria, Russia, and Turkey. They speak many languages. Some of our guests speak only their Indigenous language.

We receive a large delivery of food. The fruit disappears quickly —the cabbage and lettuce not so much. We maintain a small pantry in the kitchen. There's a bigger one downstairs with the usual large brands of packaged foods. Donations of food come in regularly from people and groups in the community.

Food donations come in regularly.

It's about time for everyone to gather for breakfast now. There's a little one fussing down the hall.

MARCH 18, 2022

On a lighter note...

Just before we are about to have lunch, I open one of the refrigerator doors. There's a stash of big bottles of Coca Cola. Hmmmm. We ask guests not to store personal items in the kitchen. I put the bottles on the counter where food and drink is passed between the kitchen and the common room. Who would claim them?

"I forgot," said the guest who had organized the lunch preparations, sheepishly.

"Well, maybe you'd like to share with the others?" I offer.

He hesitates for a long moment. Then he sighs reluctantly and agrees. The room breaks into spontaneous applause.

MARCH 19, 2022

ICE agents stop by in the morning to drop off someone we are expecting. He is in a wheelchair and says he can't get around without assistance. Yikes. It's true this time. How to get in contact with the people he crossed with? It turns out his friends—a family—just arrived at Casa Vides. They've been wondering where he is too.

It takes just a few phone calls to get everyone back together again here. One of the new arrivals can stay with our wheelchair-bound guest in the men's dorm. He'll make sure his friend's needs are met. Mom and child are assigned a private room upstairs where families stay. They'll all board a bus this evening. Our guest with the ambulatory issues will be reunited with his wife. They've been separated for a year.

Later I sit in the office using Google Translate to ask a new young Kurdish guest from Turkey a few questions. Then I call his sponsor to see about travel plans. The sponsor turns out to be a family friend who lives on one side of the country and speaks English. But our guest wants to travel to the opposite side of the country. After they talk for a few minutes, I take the phone again.

"How can I help?" are his next words.

Those words warm my heart every time I hear them. He will facilitate communications with family members and call us back with details once travel plans are made. Next, our guest wants to call his mother in Turkey. Our phone bill would be outrageous if guests used the house phone. He does have his own phone and can use WhatsApp.

He asks if there are stores nearby. His eyes light up when I say he can buy soft drinks and some smokes at a gas station two blocks away. He enjoys sitting quietly on the bench outside the house, listening to his music. I find the resilience of our guests truly remarkable. The almost complete lack of drama, given what people have been through, is inspiring.

Lunch prep is underway. I notice our injured guests pitching in by peeling and cutting up potatoes or folding dish cloths and towels.

Antony is making creatures out of balloons for the children. He leaves one in the form of a flower for an injured guest who'd been tearful the other day.

In the evening, our guest who is wheelchair-bound and his friend want to go out for a walk.

"Do we need to worry about the police?"

I suggest they bring their immigration papers along in case they are questioned. I learn that the guest with mobility issues lives with the aftermath of a closed head injury from an encounter with immigration. It isn't clear how recent that incident was, but the fear in his eyes is real. They leave to enjoy the mild evening and some privacy, and they don't go far.

This long but rewarding day is nearing an end. While I am sipping a cup of tea in our hangout space, a volunteer comes in with a smile on her face. She says that one of our young injured guests, who had moved on a few days after his surgery, just called. He wanted us to know that he'd arrived safely at his destination and was sending thanks and best wishes to everyone at the house. She says he mentioned each of us—guests and volunteers he'd come to know—by name. I will remember his warm eyes and calm, kind presence.

MARCH 21, 2022

We have curtains! And they're beautiful! Curtains are one of the finishing touches on the renovation of the house. The different fabrics were chosen to go well with the wall color of each room.

Curtains!

Spring arrived here in the desert a few days ago.

More people have been passing through our house in the past few days. We haven't had much chance to get to know them before they move on. The groups have included several people from Turkey and one from Iran. The people who come here didn't necessarily cross the border in El Paso. They are bussed in from other places like the ICE Processing Center in Otero County, New Mexico. It's impossible to understand it all. Policies seem to be inconsistently enforced. It's never clear to me why some people are immediately sent back across the border under Title 42, why others go into detention, and why some are released by authorities right away.

A PACK OF NOISY, unsupervised children is roaming the halls. I'm aware that two of our guests are recovering from surgery and would benefit from some quiet. We also understand that parents are weary from the journey and the emotional effort to hold things together. This type of ruckus is, mercifully, unusual. In contrast, a young family from Haiti with an adorable eighteen-month-old and three-year-old always sit quietly together in the common room.

The men's section of the clothes closet is now depleted with the increase in traffic. Lots of food has been delivered in the past few days. Mountains of sheets and towels are waiting to be washed. At one point, we were down to just one available bed in the women's dorm. Injured guests stay in the two downstairs dorms.

Sometimes people can get a bit lethargic and too comfortable here. These shelters are only a temporary stop. We always need to be thinking about having space available for others. Long-term guests or guests with challenging situations are assigned a volunteer advocate who checks in regularly to understand their plans and to help address special needs.

Often the situation is less than clear in the beginning. The volunteer asks questions, listens carefully, and encourages people to make difficult decisions. Occasionally, we need to point out that it is time for the guest to be on their way. The uncertainty and risks are higher for some of the guests. This case management is one of my favorite assignments.

MARCH 22, 2022

The occasional slow day is a welcome surprise. That gives us a chance to focus on neglected projects around the house, have a relaxed conversation that's not work related, and have more time to engage the guests in more creative ways.

School has started up again, which has separated the two nine-year-olds. One is in school. One isn't. They'd been having so much fun together. He is really lost without her. Our two young volunteers come to the rescue with colored chalk. Soon the sidewalks around the house are blooming with trees, butterflies, and rainbows.

One of the community volunteers, Scott, is a Jesuit priest on sabbatical. Scott is absorbed in working on a page in an adult coloring book. He says the Mass on Friday evenings to a packed house, since most of our guests are Catholic. Seeing him absorbed with the coloring inspires one of the guests to take a page for himself. It's fun to see people trying something out for the first time. It's relaxing and meditative for all of us.

After that there's a small afternoon karaoke party. The kids turn into dramatic MCs, hamming it up whenever a strange piece of equipment with two microphones is brought up from the basement. The two younger ones belt out a catchy Ricky Martin tune with great gusto.

Our guest from Turkey sits apart, unable to communicate with any of us without the help of technology. Betty, our Monday morning community volunteer, helped him connect with his parents back home. He is still in his teens.

After we finish singing, I fetch my laptop to see if a real conversation using Google Translate is possible. The pace is slow, but it works. It turns out our guest is Kurdish, from the mountainous area in the southeast part of the country. He shows me photos of his beautiful homeland on the computer. Since he enjoys spending time outdoors and is comfortable leaving the immediate neighborhood, I suggest he consider a walk to San Jacinto Plaza. After dark, when the trees are all lit up, the atmosphere is magical. He'll be moving on tomorrow.

MARCH 23, 2022

People tell stories about the relaxed atmosphere at the border in earlier days when it was easier to go back and forth.

MARCH 24, 2022

Looking around the common room at breakfast, it's clear that we have very few able-bodied people to handle the chores. Quite a few people have moved on in the last few days, including some of our injured guests whose surgery is behind them. One person volunteers to clean the upstairs bathrooms, and another will handle the downstairs ones. Floors in the common space and kitchen are routinely mopped after every meal. That isn't going to happen. Mercifully, they really don't need it.

I sweep up the remains of the children's breakfast and help dry dishes. The guest who'd offered to clean the downstairs bathrooms announces he is leaving. He's had a difficult time putting a plan together, so his departure feels abrupt. We say our goodbyes and offer hugs and good wishes before his ride arrives. The downstairs bathrooms won't get cleaned today, but we'll survive!

Another guest tells me she and her son missed their ICE check-in date in another state. Yesterday was the day. Their papers indicate you can check in in person or in writing. I call the number of the field office. It rings and rings. There is no fax number to send something in writing.

The guest decides that she wants to check in at the field office here in El Paso. Jeff has the time to take her. It should be a simple matter of officials making a note in her file. This guest's husband had already left for his sponsor to get things ready for his wife and child's arrival. It isn't clear he showed up for his check-in. My stomach twists. You don't blow off the U.S. government without consequences. You want to demonstrate that you are respectful and have fulfilled all official requests. He doesn't have a phone. I call the friend he is staying with, but no one answers, and the voicemail hasn't been set up. We're all adults here, but you hate to see people doing things that aren't in their best interest.

Someone from one of the consulates calls to schedule brief interviews with one of our families and a single guest. That will start the process for them to get passports from their home country. Getting this recognized form of identification is a big step for people.

In the midst of all the activity, a Homeland Security bus pulls up. (Gulp) Are we expecting people? I haven't seen any messages. Check again. Yes, with very short notice. When people come wearing their own clothes, it means they've been released without a stay at a detention center. This group turned themselves in right here at the bridge between Juárez and El Paso. No wonder there wasn't much notice. The two Border Patrol agents who drop the people off tell me this is their first experience. Maybe we're all making this up as we go along. When you're working at the borderlands and dealing with human lives, you learn to deal with the unexpected.

Mimi, a long-term volunteer, offers to help with the Covid testing in the parking lot and get the new people registered. The spring breeze lifts the papers we are filling out, scattering them all over. It is the perfect time for the guys who are replacing a broken bathroom window to arrive, but they just need to be shown which bathroom. There are a lot of bathrooms!

Our new guests are hungry. Of course, the noon meal and cleanup just ended, but there are plenty of leftovers. Two people from the new group offer to heat up the food I take out of the fridge. That keeps them occupied as I begin to phone their sponsors.

There's rarely a dull moment at any of our shelters these days.

Sitting in the volunteer room with a cup of tea and a new book before bedtime, the peals of laughter coming out of the common room wash over me. Later I join them. A small group is playing *Lotería*. Others are just sitting with their families. Then someone brings out the cornhole game. Then shortly before lights out, the volunteer in charge turns on the TV so everyone can see the tail end of a soccer game. That generates both cheers and occasional hisses of disapproval.

Who doesn't love a game of corn hole?

MARCH 25, 2022

Yesterday, one of the nine-year-olds came to each of us to let us know that he and his mom would be leaving today to join his father. He looked so sad. He and his partner-in-crime have been the senior young people for a while. They've become so close and play so well together. Though it may be hard to imagine, they've made this place their home. I asked if he wanted to stay here instead. He said, with great earnestness, that he did.

This morning, he is strumming the guitar as he sometimes does. His friend is at school, but they'll have some time together before he catches the bus. I help her make a card for him. She is awkward with so much emotion coming up. She offers the card to him and then rips it out of his hand, nearly tearing it apart. They have strong feelings for each other and aren't quite sure what to do with them. They are still young. I expect they'll remember this relationship for a long time.

MARCH 26, 2022

The highlight of my shift? Empanadas!

We have a new cook and sous chef. They won't be here for long, but it's given our chief cook a needed break.

There are new arrivals from Mali, Turkey, and several South and Central American countries.

Our three-year-old seems to be warming up to me again after I busted him twice for taking food upstairs.

MARCH 27, 2022

"I am looking for my sister (or my cousin or grandson). I haven't heard from her since Monday (or Wednesday or Friday)."

The calls come in.

We tell them that there is a website called "ICE Locator" where anyone can check to see if a relative or friend is being held in detention by authorities. But it takes a few days for a person to be added to the system. Keep checking.

Someone calls from a cold country after hearing that her young cousin from Ukraine will be released from the El Paso detention center on Monday. This individual speaks no English or Spanish. The caller wants to know how the process works and whether her family member can stay with us for one night. She will buy her a plane ticket for the following day. I explain that it is likely her relative and others will be released to us as part of a group. I reassure her that we call the sponsor as soon as possible after we register new guests.

But there are no guarantees. Someone who was released from detention was recently dropped off at the airport. He found a compatriot to share a hotel room with for one night. A concerned citizen called us yesterday and asked if we could help.

The fellow from Russia is still at Casa Vides. He has no sponsor. That makes things more difficult.

MARCH 28, 2022

I'd gotten to know his wife better than him in the few days they were here. She has a warm, outgoing personality and loves to cook. The empanada meal was her handiwork. He is quiet and mostly keeps to himself. But before they leave, the three of us have a conversation. At one point, he tells me he will need a cornea transplant. One of his eyes definitely looks sore.

Then he rolls up his shirt sleeve and shows me terrible, wide ropes of scars covering his arm. He explains that his injuries are the result of an acid attack, an example of cartel violence. Even his "good" eye is affected.

Another family with young children has firsthand experience of being extorted and having a gun brandished in their faces. The level of violence in the world is something I have trouble processing.

We ask our guests questions, but the questions we ask are related to their current situation, plans, and injuries (if applicable), and these questions are intended to support them. We respect their privacy and the tenderness evoked by traumatic experiences.

At the same time, many want to have their stories witnessed and respectfully held. It's always their call. And now, dear reader, you are part of that witness.

MARCH 30, 2022

A community volunteer and I are chatting in the office. We both agree that spending too much time downstairs in the ropería or clothes closet, is the most draining thing we do around here.

This is how people are dressed when released from detention.

When people are released from detention, they sport the look I'm wearing in the photo above. All new guests receive a change of clothing. Those who stay with us longer get a small wardrobe.

There are no elves here to magically put the clothes closet back in order, and all it takes is one person rummaging around to make it a mess. Right now, if you're a kid, you have the best chance of coming up from downstairs with something that makes you look cute. But somehow people seem to be skilled at finding the right thing or aren't particularly concerned.

On shift today, I spend quite a bit of time in the clothes closet. Not only is it exhausting, but you also can't hear the doorbell. And there are always other things that need the attention of the volunteer in charge.

Things work out best when you bring two people at a time downstairs. It seems like one mom with her child is going to take all morning. She will be reunited with her hubby, is expecting, and understandably wants to look nice. But do you have to examine every garment? Soon a pile of pants is heaped high on the underwear bin. As you might guess, we don't have a fitting room, so I send her to the bigger room next door where she is unlikely to be interrupted.

"Now, I need a top."

I ask her to put the pile of pants back in place first. It takes two requests before they are back in the section they belong in. And on it goes.

"Five more minutes," I say.

Then, exasperated, I tell her she has to choose. She can't. I am firm.

After that, I bring two more adult guests and one child downstairs. One is from Haiti and speaks some French. The other individual is a Spanish-speaker. Switching back and forth between languages ends up being quite the mash-up for me at times.

"Do you have a wig?"

What? Then I remember that wearing a wig is the norm in some cultures. Well, we don't have any wigs, but we do have something that will cover her hair. She is happy. One of these guests reminds me that her husband also needs a change of clothes.

"Let's do that after lunch," I suggest.

After my shift, I drive up to Scenic Drive with its magnificent view of the land, the mountains, and the sister cities. The view always clears my mind and spirit. Then I get a bite to eat. When I arrive back at the shelter, dinner is just about to be served, and everyone is gathered in the common room. I have to tell you that every single person I'd taken downstairs earlier looks terrific in their new outfits, especially the one who tested my patience. Her eyes sparkle. The vivid blue of her top contrasts with her strawberry blond hair which has been released from its long braid. She is radiant. The couple is clearly pleased with their appearance too.

I have a decent everyday wardrobe with me here. I haven't had all my possessions taken from me and don't have to put on the same clothes in the morning. Although it's unlikely I'll ever be eager to spend much time in the basement clothes closet, it is good to be reminded of the experience of many of those around me.

APRIL 2022

APRIL 1, 2022

Antony is extending his stay for a month.

Mimi is popular with the children who think she's so much fun. They're always asking for her and wanting a hug. She loves to join them in their activities and games. She's also very involved with the adults.

Mary, our house coordinator, is also from Michigan. While still in college, she came to El Paso as part of a BAE group and couldn't stay away. She's been here doing this work for over ten years and has a wealth of experience. She's calm and forgiving.

"As long as the house doesn't burn down, we're good," she says.

Guests have been known to blow out the six pilot lights on the stove because they're not used to this extravagant waste of energy in their country.

It's a big job to manage a building, a group of volunteers that comes and goes, and support injured guests and other guests who have a variety of other challenges. Mary does case management, repairs, inventory management, purchasing, decorating, and so much more. She has managed another shelter here in El Paso and another one in Juárez. It was a big effort to reopen this house last summer.

Mimi and Mary.

Allison is one of the community volunteers who takes a weekly shift. She is studying anthropology and public administration. After she's done with school, she envisions her work will be assisting people seeking refuge from natural disasters, war, famine, and climate collapse to get settled in a new home. Her stint at Annunciation House is great experience.

Allison is a student and community volunteer.

Another community volunteer who also takes a weekly shift, plans to work in public health and is also finishing up an advanced degree. He's writing a paper on PFAS, the "forever chemicals" we all carry in our bodies now.

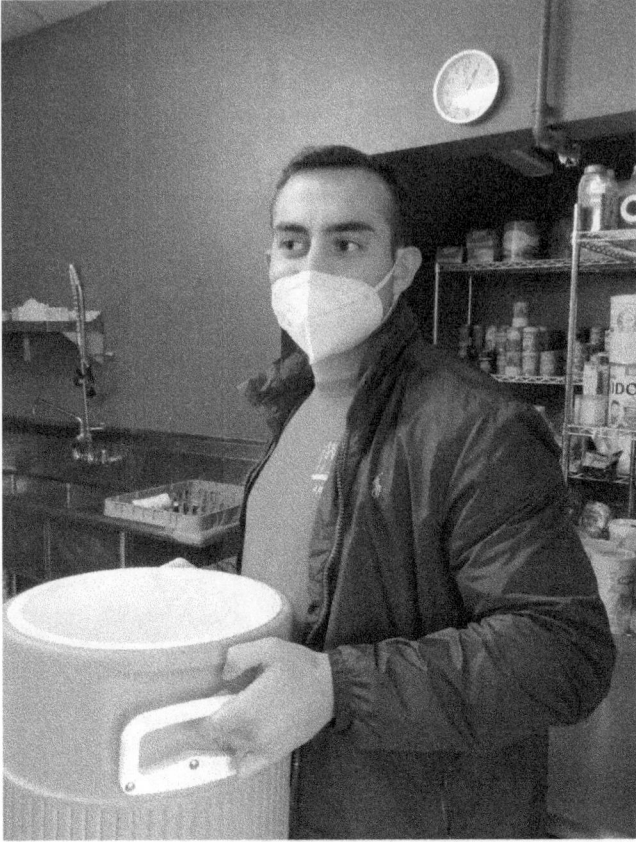

Another student and volunteer from the community is writing a paper on "forever chemicals."

APRIL 2, 2022

We've received five more injured guests in the past three days. All except one have fallen from the border wall.

APRIL 3, 2022

I've been acting as the French-English interpreter for Max, an immigration attorney, and one of our guests who is from the war-torn Democratic Republic of the Congo. I don't often have an opportunity to speak French, so it's great to find that it is still functional. Las Americas pays for an interpretation service, but it's done by phone and not very personal. You don't need to speak another language to volunteer here, but it sure helps.

Andrew is tall with a shy warmth and a smile that lights up the room. Like many of the people who pass through these doors, in the quiet hours he often picks up the guitar we keep in the common room, strumming and singing softly to himself. The first few days he was here, I would often see him gazing out the window at the sky. I knew he was worried and wondering what would lie ahead.

Because Andrew and I are both French speakers, it wasn't surprising I was assigned to be his advocate. I find myself drawn to his calm and gentle demeanor, given the many anxieties he has had to deal with. He appears to be a good candidate for asylum. He has been with us for three weeks and I've enjoyed getting to know him. He gave me permission to share his story in more detail.

French is still his country's official language, but Lingala is his native tongue. He also speaks Swahili. I've been interpreting conversations between him and Max, the attorney who got him and four other people from Africa out of the detention center. He had been in detention for nearly three months.

Andrew has no family in the U.S., but he does have a small community of friends. He tells me his father was killed in the fighting in his country. Emotion wells up in his eyes as he says he believes his mother and younger sisters are still alive, but he doesn't know where they are. He fled Congo and lived in Brazil for a time, where he continued his work in the hotel industry. At some point he headed north, losing his cell phone along the way.

I continue to interpret for him and Max, whose humanity and

commitment to the well-being of our guest touches me deeply. Max and a colleague have access to the detention center and work to get the most vulnerable people released, often because of health conditions. Andrew has asthma.

In a longer conversation with Andrew, Max asks: "Where do you want to go?"

He wants to go to a city in New England where he knows people. He is excited by the prospect of moving to a state-run shelter and is ready and eager to board a bus, unfazed by the long, cross-country journey. His friends have already raised $200 for the fare.

Then some kind of magic starts to happen.

"I used to live in that city," Max remarks. "I have friends there who might be able to help."

He suggests it might be worth it to wait a week, so he can make some phone calls. He wants to help Andrew get an interim place to stay so he can apply for funding for airfare with another organization. He agrees.

"Oh, by the way, we got Evan out yesterday. He's free."

Evan was the last of the group in detention. Andrew's face fills with delight.

"Hey, why don't I see if I can get him on the phone so you can talk to him yourself?"

Evan picks up, and a joyful conversation follows. I am watching something beautiful unfold—a supportive relationship in a community of care.

It takes a few days for Andrew's friend to transfer some of the money for the bus fare to Max so he can buy him a phone instead. Max outlines the steps that Andrew will need to go through to apply for asylum and gives him the names of a few organizations at his destination that might be able to offer practical assistance. I translate all this onto paper, so he will have something to hold on to and refer to later.

Andrew will not be able to work for six months after the application is filed. People want and need to work, so this is a hardship and puts them in a difficult position.

Max takes photos of the expired medications Andrew was given in detention; drives him to his ICE check-in; gets the venue for his court date changed to a new location; and turns in the limited-function phone he was given because it isn't working. Andrew is now delinquent in checking in with daily photos to the authorities because of the problems with the phone. Max wants to make sure all these details are noted in Andrew's immigration file.

Just before our guest leaves for the East Coast, Max stops by one last time to review details and to say goodbye. Andrew holds back tears as he expresses his gratitude to both of us. It is a moment.

Max will not be representing Andrew in his asylum case. He will need to find representation out east. It's not easy. But the courts in the northeast tend to be friendlier toward asylum seekers than here in El Paso.

Andrew's example teaches me a lot about the grace that is present when you allow yourself to experience both your inner strength and your vulnerability. I'm grateful to have gotten to know him.

APRIL 4, 2022

All work and no play is no good. So for someone who loves dancing, an evening out with the *Ballet Folklórico de México* is an energizing change of pace.

It was quite a scene outside, waiting for the doors to open. But I forgot my cell phone, so I couldn't take photos of the young people dressed in colorful traditional dresses or as mariachis. Evidently, they do performances for their schools and were there to see the show.

The dances range from envisioning what Indigenous life might have been like before European contact, to a celebration of culture, dress, and movement from different parts of the country. I leave feeling joyful and energized.

APRIL 5, 2022

Two more people come to us from the hospital today. They both fell from the border wall. Both will need surgery. Covid restrictions on immigration may be lifted on May 23rd. There are thousands of people who've been waiting to make their case in shelters on the Mexican side of the border.

We have another guest from Mexico who is here on humanitarian parole, official permission to temporarily enter the country. She is here to be with her daughter, who is in intensive care. Mom shows me a video of her daughter opening her eyes for the first time since the accident on the first day of her visit. This guest is learning the bus system so she can come and go by herself.

There's a family that arrived a few days ago with the most beautiful baby. When they're working in the kitchen, they use one of the plastic crates used to store produce as a crib. They have prepared a delicious lunch that includes some guacamole and homemade fries. Yum!

In the evening, thanks to the creativity of Antony, we play a game at the house meeting that has everyone laughing. A category is named, and one by one, everyone has to name something in that category—quickly, between claps. We cover colors, countries, flowers, and more. Repetitions aren't allowed. If you can't do that, you have to suck on a piece of lime. I take my turn at the end.

After the weekly Covid tests are administered, one of the guests gives me a look and gestures to a test card across the table just to the right of where I've been sitting. It's a positive test, a first for a guest in this house. Several volunteers from CDR recently tested positive and are isolating. The guest is taken to a private room until someone can collect her things.

APRIL 6, 2022

On shift today, I refer a number of media inquiries to our director. He lets me know a reporter from the local newspaper will stop by to interview the injured guests who came over the border wall. All but one are interested in sharing their stories. We currently have nine injured guests in the house. Three are scheduled for surgery next week.

Meanwhile, one of our airport volunteers calls to say she and a group of departing guests were harassed at the airport. Airport volunteers meet our guests before their flights to help them print their boarding passes and find their gate. Most people who stay with us are boarding a plane for the first time, so navigating the check-in process at the airport isn't clear.

I've had several conversations with a priest on the East Coast who will be receiving one of our guests after he gets his plane ticket. This guest is happy. He has no family or friends to depend on and is quite young. I am happy to see him move on too for several reasons.

A friend of a friend is volunteering for a few weeks at CDR, the converted warehouse on a street of warehouses. I stop by to say hello. It's my first time there. I help serve dinner and meet some of the volunteers. Disposable plates, plasticware, and cups are used. The shelter has about 200 guests this evening, compared with our thirty last night. It's a quick in-and-out for most people there, just one to two nights.

The pace of life in this shelter is wild. Artwork softens the large spaces, but I'm very grateful to be assigned where I am. It feels more like a home, and we manage to get to know many of our guests.

APRIL 7, 2022

I've been down for the count with a cold. So it looks like I'll wrap things up a week from Sunday the same way I did at the end of my first time at the border two years ago.

APRIL 10, 2022

I've gotten to know Mike, one of the people who lives in the veterans' shelter, over the past few months. He likes to hang out in the community garden.

I chat with him on the days I'm on laundry detail, wheeling the big tub of sheets and towels back and forth between the washing machines at the administrative house and A-house. He's invited me several times to join them for coffee and conversation on Saturday mornings, but I'm usually on shift then.

Mike has introduced me to the neighborhood cats: Cinnamon, Shadow, and Vanilla. He clearly has a feeling for them and tells me they help him stay connected. He says that a retired Master Sergeant who had lived nearby knew the multigenerational family history of about twenty cats in the area, including their personal quirks. He had many amusing anecdotes to share. Mike calls him the "catfather," and modestly admits that he sees himself as no more than an acolyte.

I take some apple peelings over to the compost pile in the community garden this morning. Don't ask me how you raise a garden in the desert, but the plants in the raised beds are coming along nicely. There are lots of metaphors here.

APRIL 11, 2022

We field a wide variety of calls when on shift. There is a notebook of community resources to refer to.

An elder calls looking for a source of food. He says it is the first time he has needed help. I chat with him for a few minutes and refer him to several food pantries.

Someone calls looking for shelter for her grandchild who lives with depression I refer her to a shelter that focuses on people with mental illness. There are other shelters in the area that focus on specific populations such as pregnant women, women with children, and farm workers.

Two people stop at the house during lunchtime. One of them is from Cuba. He knows his wife has been released from custody, and they are trying to find her. We don't have anyone from Cuba staying with us at the moment.

Someone of Ukrainian ethnicity calls from another city in Texas. He is interested in sponsoring a Ukrainian family. This is a big commitment. People need to have some understanding of all that sponsorship entails. The congregations here and in New Mexico are really stepping up to help meet shorter-term needs. It is so much easier to do this work as a community.

One of our guests was injured while sleeping in a dumpster.

Like other major cities in the U.S., there is a population of people who live on the streets. There is so much need out there. Because we are downtown, we see things that those who live in wealthier neighborhoods don't. One of our recent guests was sleeping in a dumpster when it was scooped up by a trash hauler. He ended up with a broken pelvis. He's a young man with a lot of heart. His sponsor and I share the same name. He often remarks on that.

APRIL 12, 2022

It is sad to see two of our names missing from this week's schedule. Antony was asked to lend a hand at the big house for the rest of his stay. My name isn't on the schedule either. It turns out the cold was Covid after all. I tested positive after two days of symptoms and two days after exposure. I walked the few blocks to the apartment at our administrative house as soon as I could pack a bag, joining two other volunteers from CDR who were finishing up their time in isolation.

I had been looking forward to spending my last day off in Juárez, wandering around the cathedral district and markets, buying a few gifts. That won't happen. The friend I planned to go with, a community volunteer at Casa Vides, told me she had tested positive too.

It seems to be a mild case. After two days of sleeping most of the time, I was able to enjoy two short walks yesterday. I'm able to follow up on a few situations by phone and a pile of Covid tests are waiting to be entered into the state database. My ten days of isolation ends on Friday, so I'll be able to return to A-house, pack up, and say my goodbyes on Saturday.

It's more than a bit bizarre to be ending this chapter the same way I ended my stay two years ago—in isolation in the same place with a mild cold before Covid ravaged El Paso during its first wave.

Two years ago, I was asked to make a list of food stuffs to keep on hand here for volunteers who become infected. Now I get to see how the plan has become a reality. Meeting changing conditions is nothing new for the organization. But that doesn't mean it doesn't add to the stress level of the volunteers.

APRIL 20, 2022

From our house coordinator:

"This past month has been difficult. Our volunteer staffing has been low. We've been getting between two and five people a week who have fallen from the border wall and need to stay with us for a surgery, which requires being transported to appointments and to the hospital."

Title 42 has not yet been lifted, yet the numbers this week mirror what we were seeing in 2018-2019: Monday, 453 people; Tuesday, 472; Wednesday was our peak so far this year with 558 people released.

"With the help of the community, so far we've been able to manage. But we need your help. Please come down to volunteer! Even if all you can do is make a loving box of PBJs."

Newer Murals of
El Paso

This remarkable installation looks over the San Jacinto Plaza on Mesa Street at Main. It is sixty-four feet high, an enormous and colorful depiction of a mountain lion, designed by Portuguese artist Bordalo II. It is part of a series called *Big Trash Animals*. The creature is made entirely from discarded items, including painted plastic, some old tires, a highway sign, a bike, and much more.

The Green Hope Project and other partners helped bring this colorful being to downtown El Paso.

A window to the Franklins.

I'm invited to have lunch with a community volunteer I worked with last winter and a few of his friends. On the way, I pass this vibrant new mural, *A Window to the Franklins,* by Jesus "Cimi" Alvarado. The themes of murals continue to shift over time: this one is a celebration of the land.

"It was good for me to be up there in the mountain, just painting," Alvarado said. "I was hoping that you would begin to believe that the wall wasn't there, and you were just looking through the wall at the mountain."

REBIRTH
JANUARY–APRIL 2023

You named me big river, drew me—blue,
thick to divide, to say: spic and Yankee,
to say: wetback and gringo. You split me
in two—half of me us, the rest them. But
I wasn't meant to drown children, hear
mothers' cries, never meant to be your
geography: a line, a border, a murderer.

I was meant for all things to meet:
the mirrored clouds and sun's tingle,
birdsongs and the quiet moon, the wind
and its dust, the rush of mountain rain—
and us. Blood that runs in you is water
flowing in me, both life, the truth we
know we know: be one in one another.

—Richard Blanco [1]

This is my third journey to the borderlands. The final stage of the pilgrimage is rebirth—a shift of perspective and awareness. The challenges of the journey give way to newfound personal growth and transformation.

The drive to El Paso includes a long visit with Margaret, a proud Cheyenne-Arapaho elder I had met at an Indigenous-led symposium in northern Wisconsin the prior summer. Margaret is a fluent speaker of Cheyenne and one of the Council of the Thirteen Indigenous Grandmothers. I could never have imagined that her world and the history of her people would connect with the history of El Paso and the wider history of the extreme violence it took to establish the territory of the United States from coast to coast.

Almost immediately, I find myself drawn to the title of a book I spot on an end table in her living room, *Killing Beauty in North America* by Constance Mills Atkins Buck. Margaret's name is among the acknowledgements. Constance Buck is the great-granddaughter of Anson Mills, a land surveyor who named and laid out the first plans for the city of El Paso. He commissioned the Mills Building that stands on the corner of Oregon Street and Mills Avenue opposite the San Jacinto Plaza.

Mills eventually became Brigadier General in the U.S. Army, was involved in the Indian Wars, and led the first recorded assault against the Plains Indians after the Battle of Little Bighorn. Trophies of this massacre hung on the walls of Buck's childhood home. Troubled by their presence, she returned these historical treasures to the people they were taken from and advocates for a collective reckoning with the historical and on-going genocide of Indigenous peoples in the Americas that has yet to be fully acknowledged and integrated into our collective understanding of ourselves.

Margaret and I share many intense conversations about her experiences, the Native American Church which began in the Oklahoma Territory, and the ongoing intergenerational impacts of the ethnic cleansing on her community and her people. We shed quite a few tears, healing tears. I imagine our ancestors eavesdropping on our conversations and nodding from time to time.

Connecting the dots between events to reveal larger patterns in the sweep of history would become a theme in my third winter in El Paso. The generational impacts of the violence of colonization and conquest at home—forced displacement—as well as the violence of empire abroad and its impact on immigration would continue to offer insights. I would see even more contradictions, complexities, and nuance this time.

The border city had been so much in the news before my arrival. Things had begun to calm down somewhat by the time I arrived, but there are still many people on the streets outside Sacred Heart Church, and the president is about to make a visit to the city.

Venezuela is melting down in part due to harsh U.S. sanctions. A quarter of the population is said to have fled the country. Compare this with the situation in the Ukraine where a third of the population has left. How do you take this in? Displacement has enormous implications over time for generations and centuries. Of those who have left Venezuela, around 80% are said to be remaining in Latin America and the Caribbean.[2] That means we're only seeing the minority here at the border. Even so, in my third winter in El Paso, the great majority of our guests are from this one country. Annunciation House has been renting two motels and using two of the three shelters to get undocumented people off the streets.

After the long drive and after spending two weeks in Oklahoma, I have opted for a few weeks of rest before going back to work.

To get acclimated to the current situation, I offer to work full time and live in-house for two weeks. I am assigned to Casa Papa Francisco (CPF), a recently acquired property with a lot of promise. This shelter is currently focused on hospitality for people from Mexico who qualify for U.S. Social Security death benefits; unaccompanied young people on their release from custody and foster care on their 18th birthday; and single-parent families with special needs who would benefit from calmer surroundings than the other shelters offer.

After I complete my two weeks there, I'll return to Annunciation House as a community volunteer. That means I will no longer be living in the shelter. It also means I can have a schedule that aligns with my energy level. It will allow me time to broaden my perspective with other experiences, like spending more time on the Mexico side of the border. I expect to work one shift a week with a shift partner, help with laundry, and give injured guests a ride for pre-op appointments and surgeries. People are continuing to come over the border wall. There are about double the number of guests at A-House compared with last winter.

Another A-House volunteer and I find a place to live at the Columban Mission Center (CMC), just a block away from A-House. It couldn't be more convenient. The Columbans are a Catholic order whose work with the poor and disadvantaged I respect. They organize BAE groups, staff a shelter in Ciudad Juárez, and serve a daily meal there on weekdays to people who've fled their homelands, are seeking refuge, and often sleeping on the streets. They also advocate for humane immigration policies.

JANUARY 2023

JANUARY 8, 2023

I make a trip to Sacred Heart Church to see for myself what the situation is like. To witness the scene from the wrought iron fence that separates the sidewalk from the building is emotionally draining. Red Cross blankets, duffel bags, stuffed toys, and items of clothing tucked into tree branches are everywhere. Two city buses function as warming centers. Porta potties line the opposite side of the street. A swarm of reporters and camera operators are reporting live on the day of the president's visit.

I speak with a younger individual from Venezuela who asks me for money. He says he has parents in Colorado and a wife and two children at home. I listen. We make a human connection and share a hug.

Sacred Heart Church.

Other shelters have been set up in the city. For example, the convention center which served as a field hospital during the first wave of Covid is now a shelter.

Why are there so many people on the streets? Any organization that receives federal funding is prohibited from offering shelter to people without immigration documents. Some people claim that they have been released to the streets by authorities with no papers or court date to make their case.

There are no easy answers. And there are many competing agendas and narratives.

Media prepare to cover the presidential visit.

JANUARY 9, 2023

It's my first day at CPF, which is located near a major highway in what looks like a Mexican barrio. This low volume shelter used to be a convent and a school for little people. Only the convent space is ready for occupancy. It's an attractive space. The only downside is that the kitchen and dining hall are not close to the office and the front door. I'm surprised and delighted to learn that I'll have my own bathroom. What a luxury! The school has been abandoned for years and needs a lot of work. The place has gates and secure courtyards where children can play safely away from traffic.

When I arrive at CPF, the team includes Bea and Carol, who I already know from Casa Vides. They did all the work involved in preparing the shelter for occupancy. There are two short-term volunteers who will be here for just a few more weeks. An attorney who is doing some projects with Las Americas will also be staying here for the next few months.

OF COURSE, no morning would be complete without a plumbing issue. One of our guest's rooms and part of the hall were flooded in the early morning hours.

I orient myself to the space and begin to meet our guests, including a pregnant Mom with two adorable children. Before my arrival, mom had to be hospitalized with some complications. I had heard that the younger boy was traumatized by his mother's "abandonment," added to the trauma of the journey north. At one point, he was so distressed that he ran around trying to bite people. It was upsetting for everyone. All the families here could be described as having high needs.

No morning is complete without a plumbing issue!

JANUARY 10, 2023

It is evening. He stands in the doorway while I am on shift. Something is definitely wrong. I sit him down and pull up a chair to sit in front of him, knee-to-knee.

He cries and murmurs that he is going to leave his family and go out on his own. He talks about his sadness and dreams of having his own apartment and money. If you are a parent, you've probably experienced something similar. I tell him I agree with him about the difficulties of his situation and observe that he is right about being upset—also very brave. I tell him his life is important, and we care about him.

After some time, Mom comes to fetch him and take him back to their small room where she and his four siblings sleep. He is ten years old, bright, beautiful, and very, very sensitive. He and one of his siblings wet the bed most nights.

These kids are all in school. That's a good thing. Like most people from his country, they have nowhere to go and no permission to travel to their father. Some of these families can be here with us for years.

After emotionally intense moments like this, it can be soothing to fold some sheets and towels, get some fresh night air, or just sit quietly.

JANUARY 12, 2023

I give one of our departing guests and her three-year-old child a ride to the airport. She is boarding a plane for the first time to be reunited with her husband. Like others released by authorities, they will have their day in court and may or may not be allowed to make a permanent home here. Our guest tells me a little about her month-long journey north on foot, passing through the jungle and mountains of the Darién Gap.

Two teens are dropped off by authorities on their eighteenth birthday. Young people who cross the border without a parent or guardian, like these teens, are held in immigration custody until they become legal adults. Upon their release, they usually stay with us for just one or two nights before they travel to the homes of parents, other family members, or friends.

We are also offering hospitality to a lesbian individual from Central America who is here for a court date. She is fortunate to have an attorney. LGBTQ+ people are recognized as a vulnerable population and can often present a good case for being granted asylum.

In the evening, we all participate in a fun, active after-dinner game led by one of the volunteers who used to be a camp counselor. Activities like this are simple, but they make a difference, lifting everyone's spirits from the boredom and uncertainty that weigh so heavily.

JANUARY 14, 2023

I enjoy a little getaway with Meg, one of my young colleagues, at a favorite coffee shop. After that, I drive by Sacred Heart where the situation on the streets is becoming my barometer for the flow of humanity into the city. I see that the crowds gathering there and in other locations have thinned out in the past week. We are hearing stories that concern us.

We talk about the video on Twitter that Bea had shared. It captured Ruben Garcia's eloquent, impassioned, and pointed remarks at an immigration roundtable that included a number of state senators and law enforcement officials:

"Would someone tell me that to do humanitarian work in our country is a prosecutable offense? Tell me that before you leave. That is totally unacceptable. And so we need to address that. I am extremely grateful to the Border Patrol because they have maintained a policy—a long-term policy—that says: 'We will not go into churches; we will not go into the schools; we will not go into the hospitals; we will not go into the funeral homes; and we will not go into the NGOs (non-governmental organizations, known in the U.S. as nonprofit organizations) doing social services.' We need to hear that unequivocally from the Texas Department of Public Safety that we will not do any of those things here, and we will not go after the volunteers.

"The final point that I want to make to you today is this concept of 'secure the border.' How many administrations do we go back to and the same mantra: 'Secure the border. Secure the border. Give me more money to secure the border.' When we had 2,000 Border Patrol officers decades ago: 'We need more money to secure the border.' And so we then have 10,000 Border Patrol officers. 'We need more money to secure the border.' We have 20,000 Border Patrol officers. 'We need more money to secure the border.' The truth is, that is a political ploy that we use to get votes. We've done the same thing with drugs. We declared war on drugs. 'Give me more money, more

DEA agents. We need more money, more money.' A trillion dollars later, isn't it wonderful that we can gather here today to say that after a trillion dollars, we won the war on drugs? Drugs are no longer available in our country. They're not accessible to our junior high kids because we won the war. The truth is, drug addiction is a social problem."

A few days before, there was an all-volunteer gathering at CPF which covered the risks of our work. As you might imagine, it was a lively conversation. The tension in the air was palpable. In December, the Governor of Texas, without offering any evidence, had asked the Office of the Attorney General of Texas to investigate whether nonprofits "may be engaged in unlawfully orchestrating other border crossings through activities on both sides of the border, including in sectors other than El Paso."[1]

LATER IN THE DAY, I give an Indigenous eighteen-year-old from Central America a ride to the airport. She's been with us for a few nights after being released from foster care custody. Although she speaks Spanish, the official language of her country, her mother tongue is K'iche', one of the Mayan languages.

At the entrance to the airport stands a massive sculpture installed in 2006 of the "last conquistador," Don Juan de Oñate, who established the first European settlement west of the Mississippi for Spain and served as the first governor of the province of *Santa Fe, Nuevo México*. Oñate had a reputation as a violent despot. He executed several disillusioned settlers who wanted to return to New Spain. His treatment of the native peoples was even more brutal. He was convicted in Mexico City for his abuse of both native peoples and colonists, and banished from Nuevo México. He eventually died in Spain.

The last conquistador.

The statue, installed in 2006, has stirred some controversy. It was vandalized in 2020 after the murder of George Floyd. During the same year in Albuquerque, someone defending a statue of the conquistador allegedly shot a protester as a crowd attempted to pull it down. Authorities later removed the statue.

With an Indigenous individual sitting beside me who probably didn't even notice the statue, it was almost shocking to see this vivid example of colonization, violence, and displacement lifted up in a public space. There are many other examples on the main square, at the university, and in many other places.

Our guest was flying for the first time and was nervous. She would be waiting for over ten hours in Las Vegas for her connecting flight. She won't arrive at her final destination until tomorrow morning when she will be reunited with her mother. This is more than an inconvenience. These young people are very vulnerable both on the journey north to the borderlands and until they are reunited with family members.

They are officially referred to as "unaccompanied alien children" as if they are from another planet. After their arrival at the border without a parent or guardian, these young people are placed in immigration custody. The Office of Refugee Resettlement has the responsibility for their housing and care at considerable expense, sometimes for years. Most of these kids are from the Northern Triangle of Central America, where the U.S. government has been involved in political activities that are often violent and not aligned with democratic principles. A 2019 report by the Congressional Research Service identifies high rates of violent crime, gang violence and recruitment, and severe economic insecurity as major factors motivating family members in getting these children out of the country.[2]

I could understand the need for foster care if these kids had no family here to receive them. But when there is, why they aren't reunited with them as soon as possible isn't clear to me.

These young people come to us with new clothing and a sturdy duffel bag. Providing these items is a small example of the business opportunities militarized borders offer.

I'm always left with a lot to reflect on.

JANUARY 17, 2023

Meg and I decided to spend our day off in Ciudad Juárez. I was imagining a sunny day like the ones I spent there three years ago. Today is the day.

In 2019 through 2020, there was so much life, color, and activity in the streets—despite its troubling reputation for violence—before Covid came to stay. Then, there were tables laden with irresistible beaded jewelry made and sold by Indigenous women. On weekends, the park in front of the cathedral was packed with families enjoying themselves and vendors selling foods like *elote* or sweet corn on a stick with mayonnaise and other flavors. Delish. La Nueva Central was always crowded with people from all walks of life. There used to be music here and there on the streets and dancing behind the cathedral on weekends.

But today is nothing like that. It is chilly, gray, drizzly. There aren't many people walking across the bridge. Meg has experience working in a shelter at the Mexico/Guatemala border. She points out people standing around with United Nations blankets wrapped around their shoulders or carrying a U.N. tote bag. We have lunch. There are no crowds. There are no vendors on the streets. The government recently cleared them all out. The park is now surrounded by plywood on three sides for some upcoming renovation.

After a bite to eat, we walk to the cathedral and ask to see the space downstairs where people in migration come to warm up and have a simple meal. They have the space to serve one hundred people at a time with a waiting room for the next group. Right now, they're serving around 600 people a day from 11 a.m. to 4 p.m. The faces of those serving up the soup look weary.

We both agree that we're feeling depressed by the weather and what we're seeing. It's time to go. On the walk back across the bridge, we see a few people with no laces in their shoes walking toward us, accompanied by Border Patrol agents. These are people being deported and escorted out. To see these things firsthand is different from seeing a distant scene on the news.

Morose describes the tone of the day. It clings to the clothing and the spirit.

JANUARY 19, 2023

With permission, I'm sharing a photo of one of the guests here to fulfill the requirements to get her social security checks for her husband's death benefit.

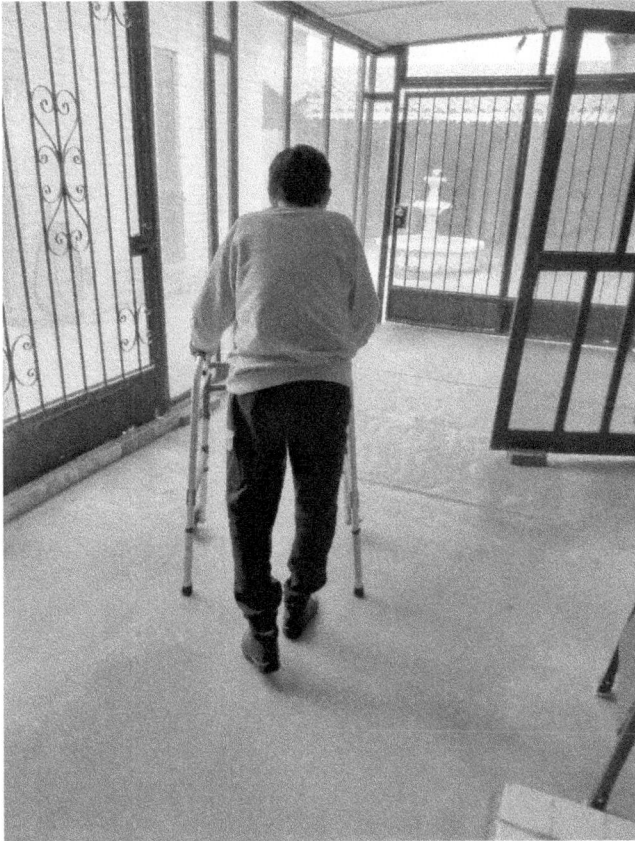

Why are these elders from Mexico required to be away from home so long to receive a benefit they are entitled to?

She gets around with difficulty with a walker. But she always shows up to help put meals on the table and clean up afterwards. She loves to share her room with the unaccompanied young people being released from custody, and we often find other guests spending time with her in her room. The new mom's baby came home today, and the three of them are bunking together. Mom seems willing but ill-prepared for motherhood.

We have another recipient of the Social Security death benefit here. She has her two teenage kids with her. They share one small room with a private bath. Nine others are signed up to spend February here at CPF.

The Social Security recipients are either elders, or they still have children at home. Their maturity and life experience helps steady our other guests. We love having them. It makes me sad and angry that they are asked to travel to the U.S. every month to sign for their checks, a financial and logistical hardship. I'm glad Annunciation House sees fit to offer them hospitality, but what happens when they become too fragile to travel? If I have time, I'd like to visit the Social Security office here to ask some questions. It's within walking distance, but there are always crowds when I walk by.

JANUARY 20, 2023

Martha's is the perfect place for a farewell breakfast. Three of us volunteers are moving on. My two weeks living in-house at CPF are complete, and I am returning to A-House. We've been quite a team with so many different skills and life experiences: an attorney, a former teacher and principal, and people with experience living and working in solidarity in the midst of profound need all over the world. Respect.

Carol, the author, Johnny, Deirdre, Meg, and Bea, the volunteer team at Casa Papa Francisco.

I pack up my things and head to the Columban Mission Center and the neighborhood I know so well.

Rose, my Filippina next-door neighbor, invites me and a few others to dinner at their house. She will be leaving soon and Beth, also from the Philippines, will be replacing her. The meal is intended to introduce her to the community and welcome her to El Paso. They serve some typical dishes from their country. I get to see some friends and meet a few new people who are doing work on the other side of the border. The conversation is lively, and it's fun to just hang out and laugh. It also feels like I've been welcomed on my first night in a new place.

JANUARY 25, 2023

Today, I'm doing the house laundry. The simple chores of daily life in a shelter can be comforting and don't involve the multitasking and energy demanded by being in charge of a shift.

JANUARY 27, 2023

It is good to be back at A-house in a familiar environment. There are about twice as many guests passing through now as there were last year. Most are from Venezuela. There are quite a few families with children, a newborn, and several pregnancies.

People continue to come over the wall. Injured people who are ambulatory are still coming to us after they're released from hospital. There are four injured guests in-house now.

There is music in the kitchen as people make lunch for all of us. Some of the guests go out to get some fresh air. We ask guests not to answer the door, so we walk back and forth to the door a lot. A family on their way to a cold country needs hats and gloves for the bus.

A company calls, wanting to sell us mattresses. A nonprofit wants to send a thousand pairs of children's shoes to El Paso. A local high school is collecting practical items to donate all semester and wants to bring over the ones we can use later in the afternoon.

I forgot a few things at CPF. When I stop by to pick them up, a doctor is there to check on the newborn and the first-time teenage mom we've been concerned about. She really needs some coaching and support. One of the moms and her children left for the northeast thanks to the group that began to sponsor families several years ago while I was working at Casa Vides. Their support includes access to an attorney, a therapist, and much more. It is easier to sponsor a family with no relatives or close friends. There are many considerations.

Relationships matter here in El Paso. This warm, generous community supports our work and the guests in so many ways. And yet increasingly militarized borders make the economy hum. There is even a brand of cigarettes called "Sheriff" and "Patrol." It's such a contradiction and a part of border culture.

Border Patrol vehicles near the Paso del Norte bridge.

Sheriff and Patrol cigarettes are just part of the culture of today's border.

JANUARY 29, 2023

Some people I know are headed to the cathedral in Juárez today to help serve the meal, so I decide to tag along.

It is a brisk morning when we walk through the segundo barrio and across the bridge. Beth and I carry a large tote bag of coats between us. Temperatures have dipped into the twenties at night for over a week now. That makes life on the streets even more uncomfortable than usual.

We arrive around 10:45 a.m. to help set up until the food arrives in large aluminum containers. I know Cristina by reputation as the organizing force behind this edible hospitality, but I've never met her. That she's done this for years is truly astounding. A meal is served on weekdays.

The guests are welcomed and briefed on the simple protocol. When the greeter asks the group how they are, they smile and say they are fine. I find that rather remarkable. A blessing is offered followed by announcements. We serve people at their tables. The first course is a thin oatmeal porridge that people sip out of a styrofoam cup. (Please save your cup for more water.) Then there is bread, spaghetti, and beans, served up in modest portions on styrofoam plates. Each group is told that if a child asks for more, they will be given more food. But there isn't enough food to offer seconds to adults. Later, an adult asks for another piece of bread. He is not denied. My eyes sting.

Once people finish, they clear their place and leave. We scurry to wipe off tables and chairs as the next group begins to take their seats on the main floor and the small mezzanine.

People are told that there are attorneys available to go over criteria for asylum and how to apply on their phones with a new app called CBP One. A computer is available for those who don't have a phone. I ask a few people who had taken advantage of this service whether it was helpful and worth their time. Those I speak with are clearly quite grateful for the opportunity. Legal help is in such short supply.

I ask my table of people where they are from: Ecuador, Venezuela, Columbia, Honduras, Guatemala. Everyone we serve today appears to be from Latin America. It's not always the case.

And there are children, too many young children. One young papa sits down with five beautiful children shortly before we leave. I feel my throat and stomach tighten.

There are many shelters in Juárez. Do they all serve meals? I know some shelters require guests to pay a modest fee to stay there. Are all the people who come here living on the street? How do they hear about the meal? How is it that other people who live on the streets in this city don't hear about it and come too?

There is no drama. Those we serve today are friendly, polite, and open to engaging in conversation. There are many cell phones, well-used. One individual whose clothing was ragged asks me for a sweater or sweatshirt. The group used to be able to help with this type of request. But for the past three months the numbers are so high, there is no time to do anything but make sure people are fed.

By the end of the afternoon, we have served over 400 people. I am exhausted and dehydrated. Volunteers don't drink a lot of water because we do not have access to the bathrooms. It's an effort for me to make the walk back home. I feel a deep appreciation for those who make this happen day after day, year after year, especially in the past few months when the numbers of people have been so high. Many of the volunteers are young people who have been in similar circumstances and are making a home in the city.

I hope to visit the cathedral regularly while I am here this winter. I'm drawn to the cross-border solidarity. It's another opportunity to treat people in a difficult and vulnerable situation with kindness and respect. Who doesn't want that?

While some people leave their homelands with the privilege of resources and connections, there is a radiance I often experience in the presence of those who have fled their homes with so little. They are so resilient, determined, and resourceful, and I can't help being concerned for them.

I don't experience that radiance among the people who roam the streets of El Paso during the night and who sleep at the entrances to abandoned stores—or the locals who line the streets of Ciudad Juárez, hollow-eyed during the day. Have they given up? They probably see us as having given up on them. There is so much need all around us.

JANUARY 31, 2023

It's always a good day when you get to hold a new baby.

After that, I drive two guests who fell from the border wall to the hospital, one for a pre-op exam and the other for wound care. Those external fixators look so grim but hold your bones in place until they've knitted themselves back together. A nurse tells me these fixators are rarely needed in her experience with U.S. residents. We see them more often than not with people who have come over the wall.

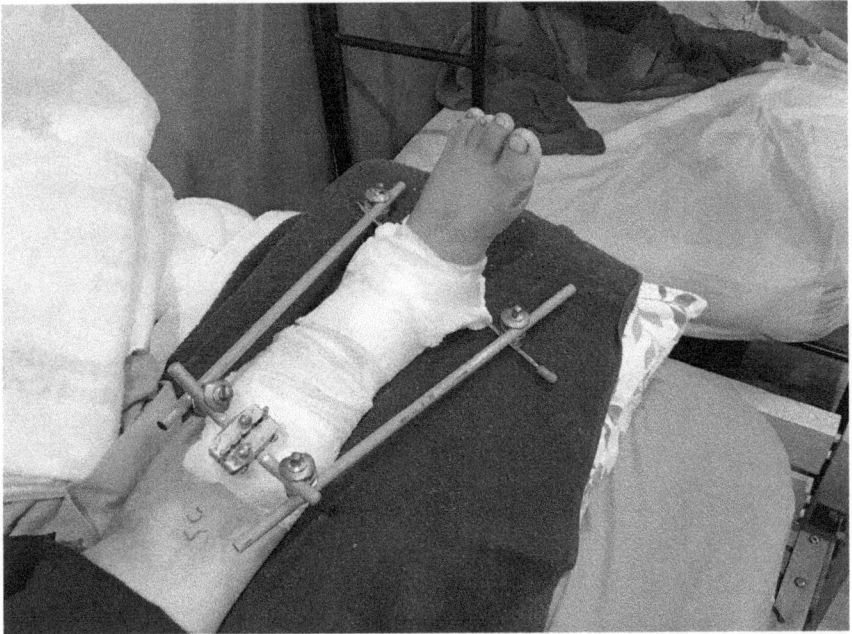

Guest with an external fixator after a fall from the border wall.

One of these guys is a long-distance truck driver with a lot of self-confidence. The other guy is younger and more tentative, but friendly. He's currently in quite a bit of pain. His fall was more recent, about a week ago. One left because of the economic situation in Bolivia. I'd never met a guest from his South American country before. For the other, violence was a motivation.

Neither of them has family here. One of them has friends in the U.S. The other has no one. That's one difference I'm seeing this winter. There are more people who do not have a sponsor to go to— people who will buy them a ticket, take financial responsibility for them, and welcome them into their home for a time.

FEBRUARY 2023

On a quite different adventure, I ride with Rita, another Catholic sister, to the far reaches of Juárez to visit *Centro Santa Catalina*. When we arrive, ten people are sewing a variety of colorful scarves, shawls, place mats and napkins, prayer flags, purses, and more in traditional fabrics. Some of them have been part of the cooperative for just a few months, others have been doing this work for over twenty years. Some of the elders who were there at the beginning have died. It is still quite cold when we arrive around 9 a.m. The space heaters need time to warm up the room. Many are wearing coats as they work. We keep ours on too.

This initiative is part of a larger nonprofit that offers a hot lunch and an after-school enrichment program for kids that includes learning to play musical instruments, using computers, and dancing. The story I am told about how this project began goes like this:

A professor was teaching social justice in higher education in Michigan. She began to question whether her classes were making a difference in the lives of anyone living in poverty. She went to Mexico and was moved by the pickers she saw swarming the garbage dump. The buildings of this nonprofit were built on part of that dump. The rest of it is fenced off. It must have been huge because it extended on both sides of the road. When I go outside to take a few photos, a fine powder from the abandoned site hangs in the air.

We are invited to join in the midmorning snack of taquitos with homemade fillings. The two people preparing lunch for the kids offer us a cup of medicinal herbal tea that tastes of cinnamon and clove. It will be offered to the students as a flu preventative.

The group sews three days a week for half a day. Everyone seems relaxed as they work. They chat occasionally and move around. Several people sew, one person irons, another does quality control and packaging. One has fingers that fly—picking threads from both ends of the fabric, and tying the traditional fringe on the shawls and scarves.

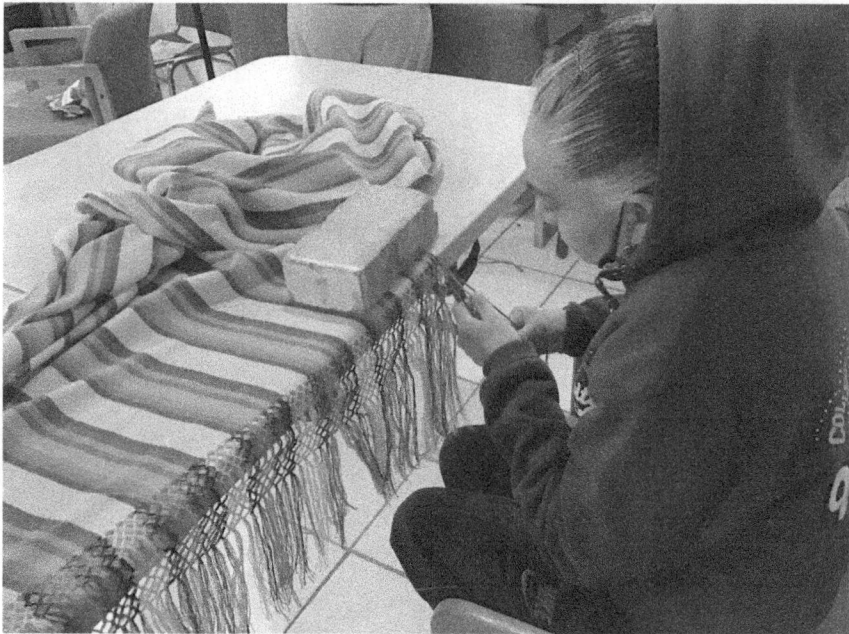

Making fringe.

The items they make will be available for sale online once some glitches have been worked out.[1] We bring two bags of items back to the attractive boutique housed at the Loretto Academy, a private Catholic school in El Paso. This sewing operation receives support from the Dominican Sisters of Adrian, Michigan.

This tiny operation contrasts with the maquilas or maquiladoras —similar to sweatshops—infamous in Juárez and other border cities.

The women share taquitos from their late morning break with us.

FEBRUARY 3, 2023

I'm grateful for a relaxing day off. I just happen to discover Gussie's Tamales and Bakery by accident after dropping off a bunch of glass at the recycling center. Nibbling tasty cheese and green chile tamales on the neighbor's patio on a mild and sunny day was such a treat. I will learn later that Gussie's has a reputation for having the best in town. Yum!

Gussie's tamales are a treat.

I SPEND the evening at the Plaza Theater, bathed and transported by the magic of Pink Floyd and a laser show.

A trip down memory lane at the Plaza Theater.

FEBRUARY 4, 2023

I'd offered to organize some family-oriented entertainment for this evening. It turned out to be perfect timing because one of the children is celebrating a birthday. I can feel the heaviness of boredom in the house. Almost all of our people are from Venezuela and most have been with us for weeks. Every day feels like *Groundhog Day*. It affects the volunteers too.

I bring in a variety of activities, many with movement for the children. Later the other guests take it from there with their own ideas. Most of the injured guests retire to their dorms. Others drift outside to get some air or walk to the Circle K to buy a Coca Cola or chips. The rest of the adults and kids who aren't participating look like they're having fun watching.

Everyone picks up the Elm Dance easily. It's a circle dance where we all move together as one. I am tickled that one of our young injured guests who gets around in a wheelchair is willing to be at the center. She makes her own circle with her chair.

We have a new Kurdish family with several children, including one with special needs who is in the hospital accompanied by Mom. Because of the cultural differences, I'm not sure Dad would be comfortable letting the other children participate in the fun, which included some dancing to a Latin beat. It's lovely that he doesn't object. Everyone has a great time, and a toddler from another family clearly has her moves on already.

At the point where I need a break, one of the dads organizes several enthusiastic rounds of musical chairs.

I walk the block back to my home away from home in the silvery light of an almost full moon with a joyful heart. I experience a lot of pleasure and even excitement when people come together across boundaries of geography, culture, language, religion, ethnicity, historical divides, and much more.

FEBRUARY 7, 2023

I take a couple of our guests to wound care and pre-op today. I've become friends with a thoughtful gentleman from India who volunteers at the hospital. It's always a pleasure to chat with him as he pushes our guests in their wheelchairs down the long corridors.

FEBRUARY 9, 2023

Oh, my goodness, this is truly turning out to be one of those days.

My morning shift begins at 6 a.m. I appreciate the few hours of grace before the activity begins with the children leaving for school. I do a round of pain medications for our injured guests before everyone shows up for breakfast.

I take out some trash after breakfast and come in the wrong door. That sets off the fire alarm. I make things worse by pulling the wrong switch. In just a few moments, a fire truck with its siren blaring pulls up to the door. Four kind people get out of the truck and come to the door. They know just what to do. I'm red with embarrassment, but they don't seem to mind. Then our director calls to make sure the place isn't on fire. I am cringing.

I hear the child of the Kurdish family will be discharged from the hospital this afternoon. So I don't understand why Dad wants to go back to the hospital with the three other children. Of course, Google Translate gives us a way to communicate, but I'm here to say that the Turkish to English translations need some work and can lead to even more confusion, sometimes quite funny. My shift partner has a driver lined up before our guest understands he can just wait for his family members to arrive. Unfortunately, there wasn't time to notify the driver before he showed up.

An ICE agent rings the doorbell to drop off a Kurdish family of four. At first, I think these must be the family members from the hospital. But where did two more kids come from? I missed the text that we would be receiving another Kurdish family. Mystery solved. We don't have a private room for another family, so my colleague on the p.m. shift set up cots in the chapel.

We have about twice the number of people in-house now compared to last year. The decibel level is higher, and there are so many requests. I try to focus on one thing at a time while making notes of who else needs what. In between all of this, I find a few minutes to cuddle this little one.

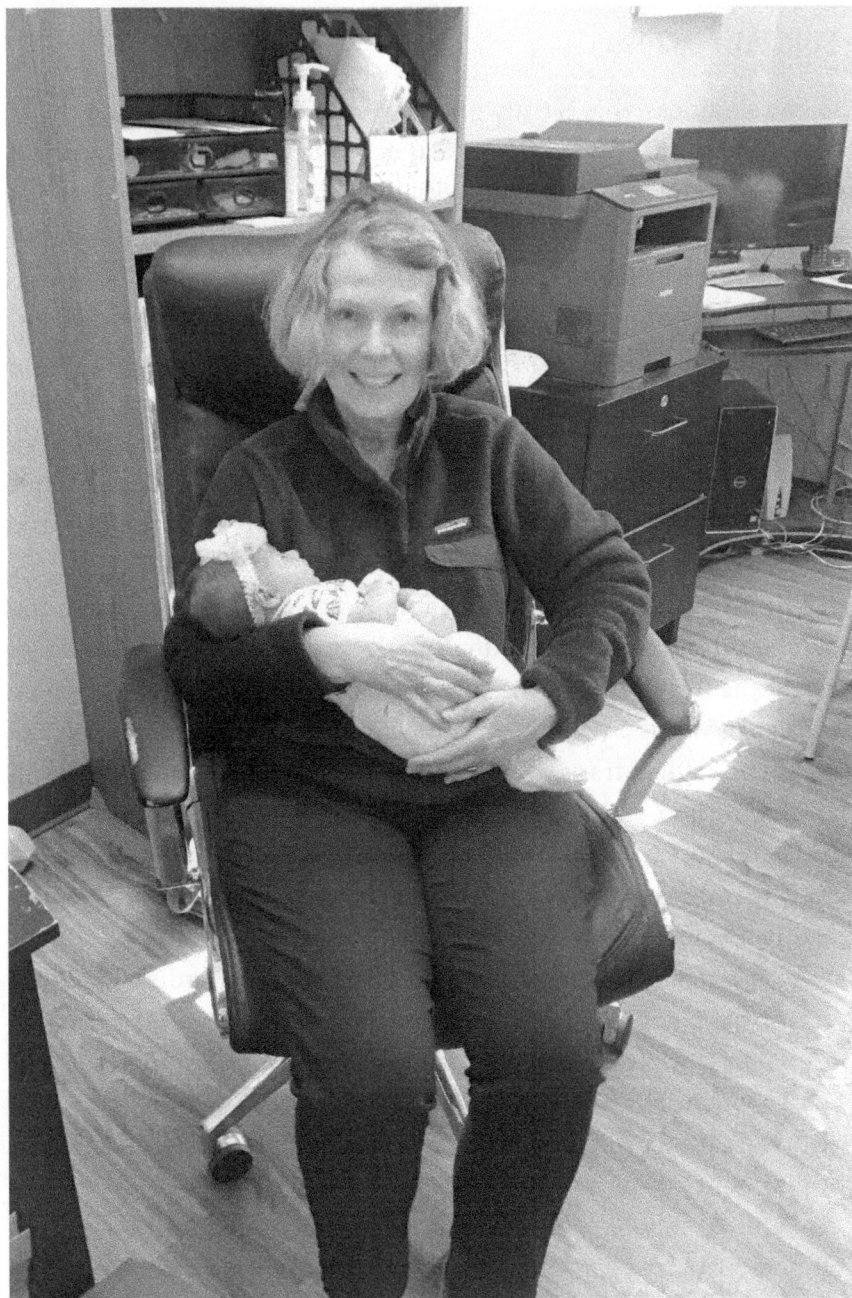

Deb and baby.

I end my workday by driving one of our guests to the airport. There is no time to line up another driver, and I'm happy to do it. Like many of our guests, he is quite nervous about his first short flight. He is lucky. His injury from a fall off the border wall didn't require surgery. He'll get around with a boot and crutches for a while.

What a day...

FEBRUARY 12, 2023

I appreciate the intention of the CMC to be mindful of water consumption in a climate where it so seldom rains. The building's electricity needs are provided, in part, by rooftop solar panels. There is no central heating or air conditioning. Nights in the high desert are quite cold, so I have a space heater in my room and often wear my coat when going to the kitchen! There are space heaters there too, but it takes time and energy to warm things up.

The Columban Mission Center.

My favorite coffee shop is just a few blocks away. From here I can also walk to the main square, the segundo barrio, the shelter where I worked three years ago, and to Mexico. I won't be walking much for the next few days though. I managed to twist my knee yesterday.

The large house hosts a variety of events, including monthly BAE groups. The groups sleep here and have full days venturing out into the community to help them understand the dynamics of the borderlands. It's fun chatting with them and hearing what they find most interesting and surprising. They bring life to our quiet house.

The organization also owns the house next door which has a nice little patio where I can sit in the sun or hang out laundry. Rose has been living there for quite a while but will be returning to the Philippines at the end of the month. She is fun-loving with a particular fondness for karaoke, good food, and hiking. People are always stopping by. She is active with the Magoffin Community Garden and good friends with the veterans who have taken responsibility for its care. These vets live in transitional housing on the next block. We can compost our fruit and vegetable scraps in the garden. I continue to be amazed that food can be grown in the desert.

Beth, the new resident, will be here for just a few more days before heading to Bolivia for an intensive Spanish language immersion program. She won't be back until August. I'll miss these congenial neighbors, but my housemate from the U.K. will still be here until I head for home.

FEBRUARY 15, 2023

My shift this week is totally different than the whirlwind of last week. The days are growing longer, and it's no longer pitch dark at 6 a.m.

The volunteer who covered the overnight shift made sure I have her number, so I can text her if I need help before my shift partner, Dan, arrives at 9 a.m. I still can't go up and down the stairs easily, though my knee continues to heal.

I'm enjoying working with Dan. He is a new bilingual professor at the University of Texas at El Paso, a hubby, and father of two. When things are quiet, he likes to get the kids off their parents' cell phones. It's a sweet scene seeing him read to one of the children who clearly loves being with him.

At least three of our guests will be moving on to their sponsors next week. Both Kurdish families have left. One of our injured guests who came over the wall decides to return to his home country after surgery. He has no family or friends here.

There are several new arrivals to meet. Our little baby is three weeks old now. She is so calm. I'll be taking Mom to her ICE check-in later today.

Lunch is easy, with lots of leftovers that just need to be heated up. During cleanup, I am drawn to some captivating music drifting out from the kitchen. I decide to join the party and help dry dishes.

One of the new guests, assigned to clean up the dining room, is away. The rest of us fill in to get the job done. We log this type of thing in the shift notes for follow-up. It can take a few days for new people to get clear on how the house operates.

Our high school student asks to bring a friend in to hang out in the common room. I check with our house coordinator. Consistent boundaries are important. Mary says a short visit is okay.

My Spanish seems to have deteriorated since last year, maybe because I'm not as immersed in the language this time. The

Venezuelans speak so fast, and their Spanish is a bit different than what I'm used to. I miss the casework I did last year when I lived in-house. I am still finding my way with a different role and adapting to a very different situation.

In the evening, I zoom in to a timely presentation sponsored by the Ann Arbor-based Interfaith Council for Peace & Justice, "Venezuela's Journey from Hope to Heartbreak: An Inside Unfinished Tale." The presenter, Lisa Sullivan, is known to some of my friends here. Lisa shares her story of thirty years of living and working in Venezuela. She served as the Latin American Coordinator for the School of the Americas Watch. (The SOA is the training institute for Latin American military and police forces mentioned earlier. It continues to operate as the Western Hemisphere Institute for Security Cooperation at Fort Benning, Georgia.) Lisa confirms in vivid detail what our guests and the people I occasionally speak with on the streets tell me.

This context is from Lisa's presentation. The exodus from Venezuela is said to be one of the largest mass migrations in history. Most of our guests at the moment are from Venezuela, and when I help serve a meal in Juárez, it's the same.

Lisa speaks of Black Friday when the currency was devalued in 1983, leading to the destabilization of what had been a strong economy. In 1989, thousands were killed when the military was sent into the streets to quell protests after fuel price hikes.

After that, there was a new constitution approved by a popular referendum in 1999, a new government, and some vibrant years. Investments were made that improved the overall quality of life. People gained a sense of what they could accomplish by working together in their communities. With another change in government, the economy is in shambles. Inflation is rampant. Money is worthless. Violence is everywhere.

Venezuela has the largest proven reserves of oil in the world, and the entire economy was focused on oil with little investment in agriculture and other industries. The country became dependent on importing food from other places. Lisa says the U.S. sanctions have added to the harm that caused the economy to collapse. These sanctions initially targeted individuals and entities for criminal and corrupt activities and were expanded to include broader financial sanctions, sectoral sanctions, and sanctions on the government.

In 2017, food suddenly disappeared from the shelves. She says she saw her neighbors' weight begin to drop ten, twenty, forty pounds. Her family and her neighbors pulled together to survive by raising as much of their food as possible. She gives thanks to the generosity of the fast-growing banana plant. Electric service was interrupted every other day.

In 2020, Lisa says there was *no* cooking gas, *no* electricity, *no* water, *no* internet, *no* cash, *no* gasoline, and *no* way out of the country except on foot.

Last spring the U.S. government announced that the lifting of sanctions would be tied to Venezuela directing a portion of oil exports to the United States. Late last year, Chevron was granted a license to resume oil production.

Currently, there is a program that allows up to 30,000 Venezuelans to be admitted to the U.S. every month. People must apply from Venezuela, pass a background check, and have a sponsor. Those who qualify are allowed to stay and work in the United States for a period of two years. Then what? She observes that the program is largely meaningless since there are no significant Venezuelan communities here to sponsor most of these people. (It is still possible for people to apply online for asylum, and people are doing that).

Lisa tells us that Venezuela had been a country of hospitality with many foreign workers. She says it was not a country that people would choose to leave. As is typically the case, the business people and professionals left first. Now for those traveling by foot, it takes around three months to walk from Venezuela to the U.S./Mexico border. We have met many of them.

In the last two years, things have gotten a little better, but Lisa felt compelled to return to the U.S. with her Venezuelan husband. Their family is now scattered in five different countries as a direct result of the hardships they've experienced.

FEBRUARY 19, 2023

I am discovering more contradictions and complexities.

I've been wanting to visit the privately funded Border Patrol Museum and finally had a chance to do it.

The Border Patrol Museum.

The museum includes displays of weapons and narcotics seized along with weapons, vehicles, and surveillance used. Those who died while on duty are honored. How the work has been portrayed in films, posters, and books is also included.

The BAE groups often have a conversation with a border patrol agent as part of their program. "What do you think of us?" is sometimes the first question, a great conversation starter.

The government sector is the largest employer in El Paso. That includes agencies such as ICE, Border Patrol, and much more. The military alone accounts for one in every sixteen jobs.

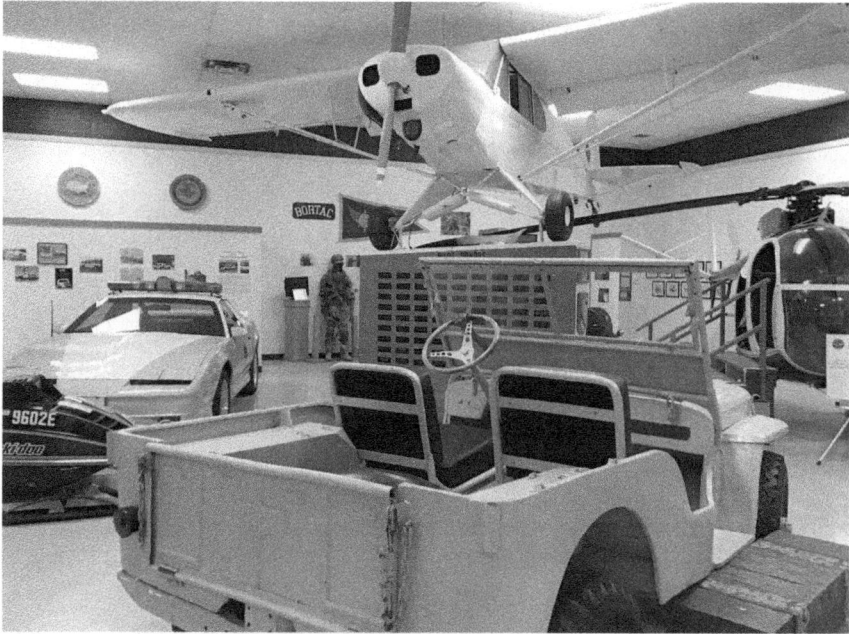

Inside the Border Patrol Museum.

Honoring the fallen.

A little drizzle fell from the skies last night. The land replied with the first poppies and cactus fruit. Spring is on the way!

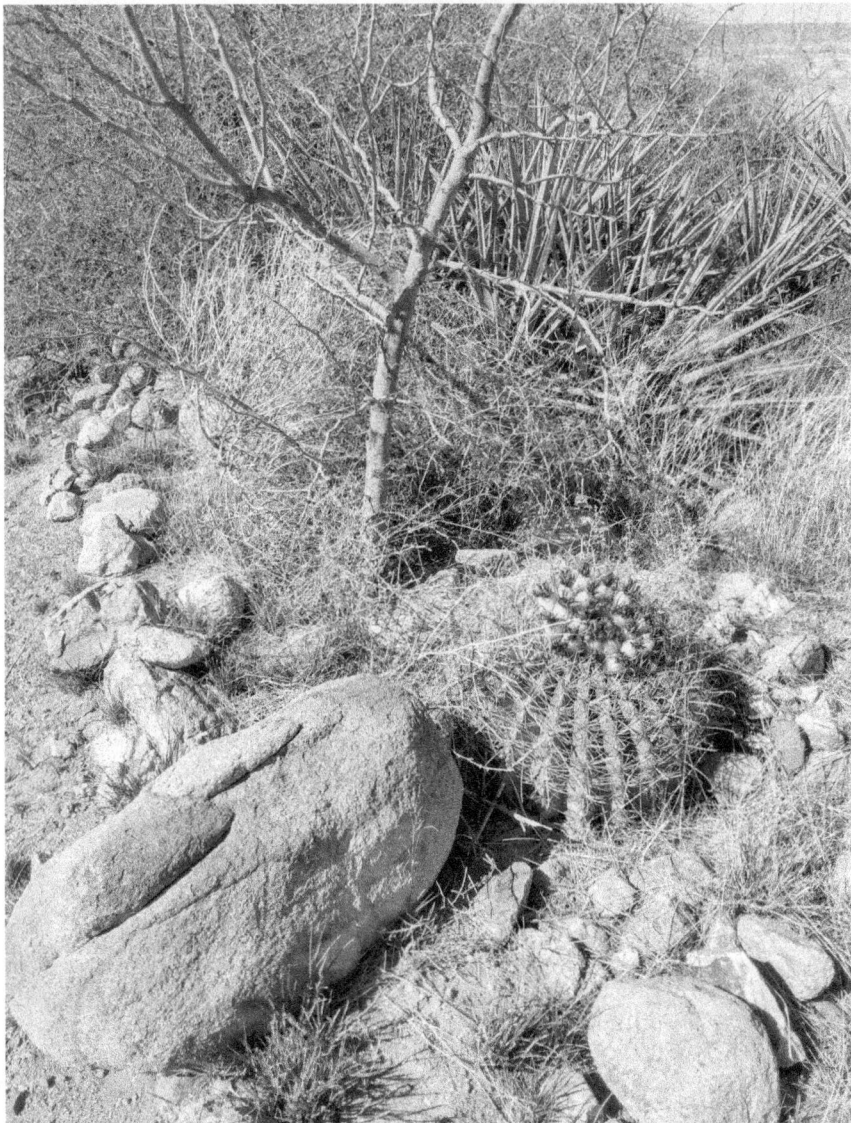

Spring is on the way!

FEBRUARY 21, 2023

It's my first time driving a guest to a check-in at the ICE field office.

I look up the address on the internet in advance, but our guest's immigration papers show a different address, the one we're familiar with. It's usually impossible to reach authorities by phone, so I have to assume the paperwork is correct.

Off we go—Mom, baby, and me. On arrival, the security guard tells us we have to go to the location I'd found on the web, so we head out of town into the desert. The road eventually turns into a massive new multi-lane freeway system with access roads under construction.

The new buildings are spread far apart from one another: a new Armed Forces Reserve Center, the Army National Guard, and a federal building that houses the new ICE field office. Militarized borders are clearly a growth industry.

We never leave the small room at the entrance to the building. One of two individuals on duty stands off to the side next to an X-ray machine. Another pulls out a chair and apologizes that there is only one. I motion for Mom to sit.

A third person comes out of another room and asks our guest for her papers, a current address, and phone number. Then she leaves the room.

The baby starts to fuss. Mom begins to nurse. We wait. The baby starts to fuss again, and Mom nurses her again. I ask the guard if he has children. He says he does. He asks if there are shelters all along the U.S./Mexico border. I say that there are. There are shelters all over the world.

The employee with our guest's papers comes out again and returns them. Mom is told she will have to come back in less than two weeks.

MARCH 2023

MARCH 1, 2023

Just when you think you've seen everything...

One of the new families brought their dog with them all the way from Venezuela. I don't know how this happened. Did they make the entire journey by foot as so many do? We can't accommodate pets, so Dad and the four-legged are sleeping outside. When I complete the security check of the building, I see a human form under some blankets along with a paw poking out.

The morning shift begins with some intensity. Another mom had arrived the day before with a two-day old baby and a two-year-old. She was in quite a bit of pain after a C-section. Negotiating the stairs to the second floor where we usually put families is hard for her, so I make up a bed in the women's dorm on the ground floor while the volunteer on the overnight shift gives Mom some over-the-counter pain medication.

Not so fast... Our one-month-old in the next bed had been up all night with the flu. One of the vacant volunteer rooms turns out to be the best bet. The two-year-old shows signs of major anxiety whenever Mom is even briefly out of his sight. He'd been taken away from her by authorities for two days while she was in labor and delivering her new baby. The trauma from experiences like that, even with the best of intentions and care, can last a lifetime. We hope she will be able to join her husband soon.

A long-term guest and her two children leave to be reunited with her husband. Seeing families get back together is a heartwarming thing. A cluster of guests surround the vehicle to see the family off, with one of the toddlers in tears.

A representative from an organization focused on transgender people calls to see if we can accommodate someone they've been advocating for. We refer all requests for shelter to our director who always seems to come up with some key questions we haven't asked.

A medical team visits the house mid-morning and meets with the injured guests. I remember our house coordinator talking about her dream of having access to such professionals last year. And now, thanks to a collaboration between Texas Tech, a local university, and Doctors of the World—an international health and human rights organization—it looks like it's going to happen! I get to have a chat with Danny, the doctor we could always count on to look in on sick kids when I was working in one of our other shelters.

We welcome two new people, including someone all the way from Belarus. She left her home a year ago and is only with us for a few hours before her husband and son who live in El Paso come to pick her up. Joy is written all over their faces.

It's a full day with so much teamwork. This team extends well beyond the shelters. People don't forget. I am told that one of our former guests stopped by recently with a big check made out to the organization.

I spend a relaxing evening with a friend from Michigan who is passing through the area.

MARCH 2, 2023

A fierce wind is sweeping sheets of wet, heavy snow through the streets this morning. We will not go to Juárez today. Traffic will be slow and heavy on the bridges. We trust the local volunteers will show up to serve the daily meal at the cathedral. I am seeing the families waiting in line for a few moments of respite in my mind's eye.

The snow is a shock. Last Sunday was mild and sunny. Spending some time in the natural area near the Archeological Museum, I saw signs of a desert returning to life all around me. The shadows on the mountains changed moment to moment as the sun moved across the sky, their huge fingers reaching deep into the ground. The poppies turned their shining faces to the light; the hills, rimmed by the ever-present signs that warn of danger from an abandoned artillery range.

The friend I usually ride with and I do end up going to the cathedral after the morning snowstorm ended, arriving later than usual. Media from El Paso are there when we arrive. I don't think much of it. As things begin to slow down by mid-afternoon, Bill, a Columban priest based in Anapra and head of the Columban organization here, asks me if I know what happened there on Tuesday and Wednesday. I have no idea.

Evidently on Tuesday, police burst into the cathedral without a warrant and aggressively forced their way into the dining area where the meal is served, trying to arrest three young men they accused of stealing. Cristina and one of the Sisters were holding onto the young men and refused to let the police take them, meanwhile a female officer shouted at Cristina, "*Pinche perra. Te voy a matar!*" or "You fucking dog! I'm gonna kill you!" On Wednesday, things turned uglier still, when the police entered the cathedral, again, and dragged a woman out by her hair, blood dripping on to the cement outside as they threw her into the back of one of the police trucks and took her away. There were three arrests after that. That's why the media is here today.

Houses of worship are usually respected by authorities as sanctuaries. Needless to say, the arrests were disturbing to everyone from the director of the program, whose life was threatened by an officer, to the volunteers and those who come to eat and get off the streets for a few moments of peace and quiet. There are always children present.

We are told that conversations are underway among authorities, the leadership of the cathedral, and Cristina to make sure this doesn't happen again.

Just last Sunday, *El Diario*, the major newspaper of Ciudad Juárez, ran a piece that asserted that the National Institute of Migration has allowed federal agents and local authorities to commit robberies, extortion, and other human rights violations against people in migration seeking refuge and a better life.

MARCH 4, 2023

The dog who traveled all the way from Venezuela with her family turns out to be a puppy. I get to meet *Coqueta* or Coquette this morning when I stop by to take one of our guests to his pre-op appointment. She and Dad are still sleeping together outside the shelter.

Meet Coqueta.

MARCH 5, 2023

I don't go to many plays, but I'm so glad I decided to ride the streetcar to the beautiful UTEP campus to see *Heroes and Saints* by Cherrie Moraga. It is powerful, beautiful, and wrenching. I am in tears at the end, and when the players come out to take their bow, they are all in tears too.

The play takes place in the 1980s in a town in the fertile San Joaquin Valley of California. This land supplies the produce served on many of our tables in winter. The play focuses on the deaths of the children of the people who work on these farms from a variety of diseases connected with the intensive spraying of toxic pesticides. People started to hang the bodies of their dead children on crosses.

During the intermission, I have a chat with a few people from Texas RioGrande Legal Aid who are staffing a table. One of them says he is concerned that people from countries like Venezuela who end up here are particularly vulnerable to exploitation because they don't have established communities in the U.S. We hear stories of people who do day labor and aren't paid for their work. We hear stories of people who've been trafficked over the border for their labor. We know that industries like slaughterhouses were hotbeds for the Covid virus. We know the reputation of the maquilas south of the border and more...

Every day I have a chance to broaden my perspective. I get to take a hard look in the mirror and see how my comfortable way of life is made possible by the exploitation of my fellow human beings, other beings, and the land. I get to see examples of the violence of increasingly militarized borders—and how wealthy countries create and protect wealth by exploiting poor countries. While seeing these things up close can sting and burn, I'm grateful for this time of reckoning. Considering how stuck we are and the poor quality of our relationships with one another and all that we depend on for life, it seems to me that the only way forward is together.

MARCH 8, 2023

My shift at the shelter is calm this week. Things no longer feel like *Groundhog Day*. A number of our guests have moved on. Some have decided to return to their home country. We're back to seeing new faces. I am grateful for the movement we're seeing.

MARCH 9, 2023

There are no police at the cathedral in Juárez today. I notice that there is no more coffee being served to the guests. After serving the afternoon meal, we drop off a massive bag of beans and another of rice at the shelter that Annunciation House briefly opened when the MPP was in effect. The house is now managed by the Columban Border Migrant Ministry. The guests prepare the food we serve to people downtown.

After that stop, we easily find the mural painted by artist Isabel Cabanillas. Both the mural and the act of violence continue to haunt me. Te observan. They are watching you. Remembering is honoring.

Our trunk isn't searched this time as we cross back, and the Border Patrol agent is respectful. There is no interrogation this time.

MARCH 6, 2023

I take a tour of the birthing center just up the street. *Maternidad La Luz* offers a modest homelike setting with two birthing rooms and the possibility of choosing a water delivery. Midwives-in-training come here from all over the world to do their field placement. The documentary *Catching Babies* was filmed there. I've been invited back to shadow a midwife for a twelve-hour shift.

MARCH 10, 2023

I take one of our guests who'd fallen from the border wall to a pre-op appointment with her young adult daughter. These appointments are usually routine. But we end up in the emergency department immediately after. Her thigh has been oozing a bloody liquid where the external fixator stabs into her flesh. After waiting with them for some time, I leave and tell them I'll check back with them later.

She was finally admitted later that evening with an infection that required IVs with three different antibiotics. Her hospital stay will be at least four nights, and her surgery may need to be postponed.

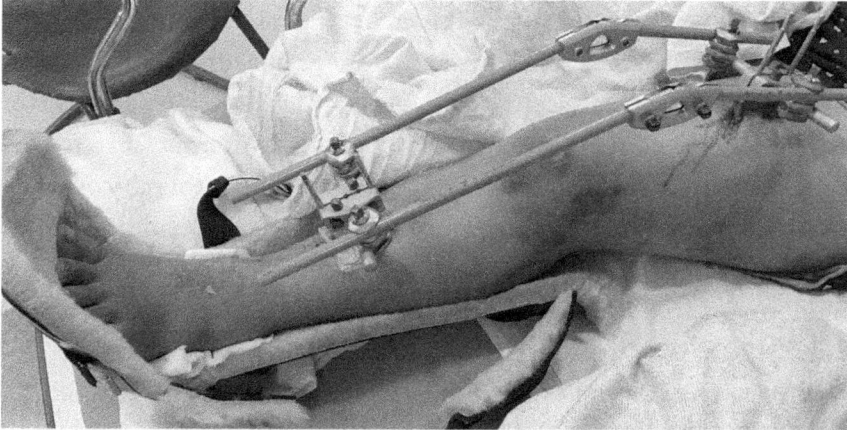

A guest has developed a nasty infection.

MARCH 11, 2023

I stop by the hospital again to see how mother and daughter are doing. I suggest that the girl might want to go back to the shelter with me to take a shower and change clothes. Mom looks panicked at the thought. It takes another day for Mom to let her leave for a few hours.

Our guest asks her daughter to take photos of her leg to share. I ask permission to do the same. I want people to be able to see for themselves.

At the house, we also receive a guest wearing a neck brace who was involved in a rollover accident. There was probably a chase, and the vehicle was probably being driven by a coyote or smuggler.

There have been a number of high-speed chases on the streets of El Paso in the news lately, all involving the Texas Department of Public Safety. Our house coordinator did an internet search that came up with seven articles describing car chases in this city over the past two months. It's a dangerous practice and can result in crashes in residential neighborhoods with vehicles speeding at 100 miles per hour or greater. Chases can be started by undercover officers in unmarked cars with no sirens or lights.

These chases aren't new, but their frequency is. I remember the fatal car accident just a few blocks away from the shelter where I was working three years ago. We received a sister and brother upon their release from hospital. The coyote didn't make it. Last year, a young father of six was chased on foot onto an interstate highway and hit.

I saw a digital sign on one of the freeways yesterday warning drivers to "watch out for pedestrians." Surreal. Helicopters leave every morning from Fort Bliss. I've seen police vehicles stationed on either side of the entrance to the zoo for the past few days. It's not clear why.

I'm not here to justify or criticize the choices people make. Maybe we all do what we feel is in our best interest. I take instruction from the Golden Rule. I also want to understand more of the context, to get to the heart of things. It is my understanding that increasingly militarized borders are a form of violence that spawns other forms of violence and corruption, including organized crime. The expense involved is enormous, and the cost is much more than financial.

MARCH 15, 2023

My shift this week is a blur.

Many of the nineteen new guests who arrived yesterday are making their travel arrangements today. There are so many details to keep straight as more people come and go again.

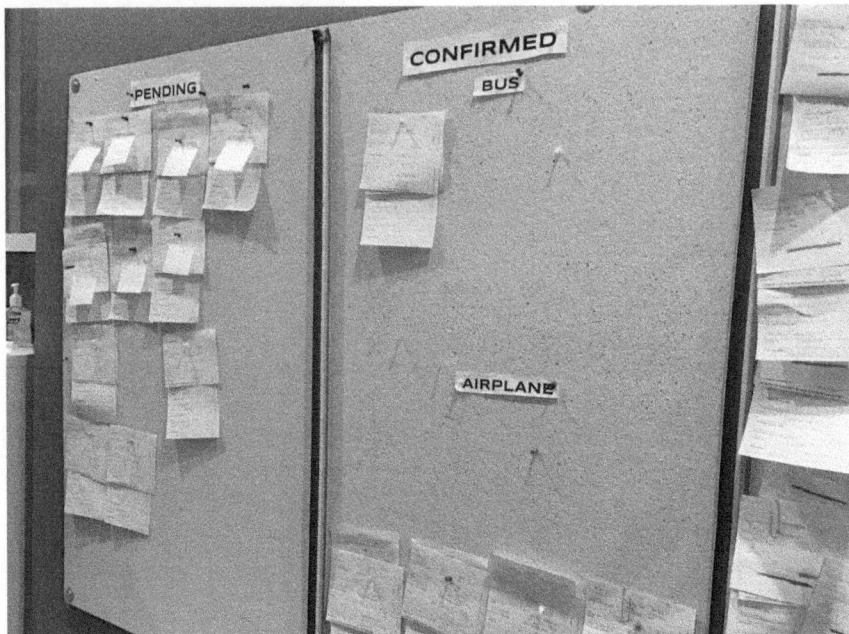

The travel board.

We ask that beds be stripped and sheets and towels brought to a big container in the common room. Update bed charts. Line up drivers. Notify airport volunteers. Make sure the rooms are clean for the next arrivals. Make sure meals are put on the table, leftovers are used up, and cleanup happens.

Answer the phone. Open the door. Respond to requests. Accept a delivery of fruit. Log follow-up items or concerns in the shift notes.

Pack snack bags appropriate to the situation of those leaving. Make a bigger one for the one who is returning to his home country.

He'll be on a bus for three to four days. A guest asks me to call a shelter on the East Coast to see if there is room for him and his children before he buys bus tickets. Yes, there is space, but they'll be bussed to Washington, D.C. where they will sleep with others in a big common room for three days and then be transferred to more private conditions. He's good with that.

Danny now stops by each week to look in on our injured guests. The individual who had the bad infection is still in the hospital. Her surgery will be moved up.

We have quite a few people from Haiti, so I get to dust off my French again. People who made their homes closer to the border with the Dominican Republic often speak Spanish. I meet some who speak only Haitian Kreyòl.

I continue to be challenged by Venezuelan Spanish. Someone wants to tell me a funny story. Those around us laugh at the right moments. I understand not one word, but it still feels good to laugh along with them.

There is another new baby and a cute two-year-old with big eyes. A new arrival from Venezuela is only with us long enough to shower, have a meal, make a phone call, and shed some tears before she is leaving for the airport. I got word to expect her two hours after she was dropped off. At least it wasn't twenty-five people getting off a bus.

With my shift partner away for the second week and with so many people in the house, I am wasted.

MARCH 16, 2023

The house where I am staying has hosted several BAE groups this month. When I was working full time in the shelters, I never had time or energy to hear any of the presentations these young people are offered. But this winter I've been taking advantage.

I'd heard good things about writer, musician, and microhistorian David Romo. David's study and writing focuses on the borderlands and the sister cities of El Paso and Ciudad Juárez. (Check out *Ringside Seat to a Revolution* and *Borderlands and the Mexican American Story*, for example.) The approach of a microhistorian is to examine small details that reveal larger insights along with the texture and quality of life in another time.

Like so many people here, he has both Indigenous and Spanish ancestry. Much of what he presented to us had to have been painful to research and speak about. He asks everyone at the end of his talk how we feel about what we heard. Whether it was sorrow, anger, or gratitude to know what happened, it was clear we all felt deeply moved.

David reminds us that people were able to travel back and forth across the river with two names freely and without a passport until 1917. One of the things that strikes a chord is learning more about Carmelita Torres, who is compared to Rosa Parks.

The year is 1917. Imagine you are seventeen years old, a maid living in Juárez and cleaning homes in El Paso. You ride the trolley across the bridge to get to work. Before you are allowed to enter the U.S., you must go into a building where you are required to strip and take a bath in gasoline. Your clothing is treated in a steam dryer.

Both of these procedures are said to be intended to kill any lice, carriers of typhus, on your body. (There were outbreaks in several cities in Mexico.) You never learn that you've been secretly photographed in the nude. Your photo and others are now on display in a bar. What do you do?

Carmelita Torres decided she'd had enough. She convinced thirty other women in her car to refuse the process. Once they began their demonstration, they were eventually joined by thousands, blocking entry into El Paso. The police were unable to break up the protest. Carmelita Torres was never seen again after her arrest.

This moment in history became known as the Bath Riots. These practices continued for decades, long after the typhus scare was over. Ongoing disrespect and humiliation take on new forms over time.

The person in the photo is David's aunt who told him stories about the steam dryers.

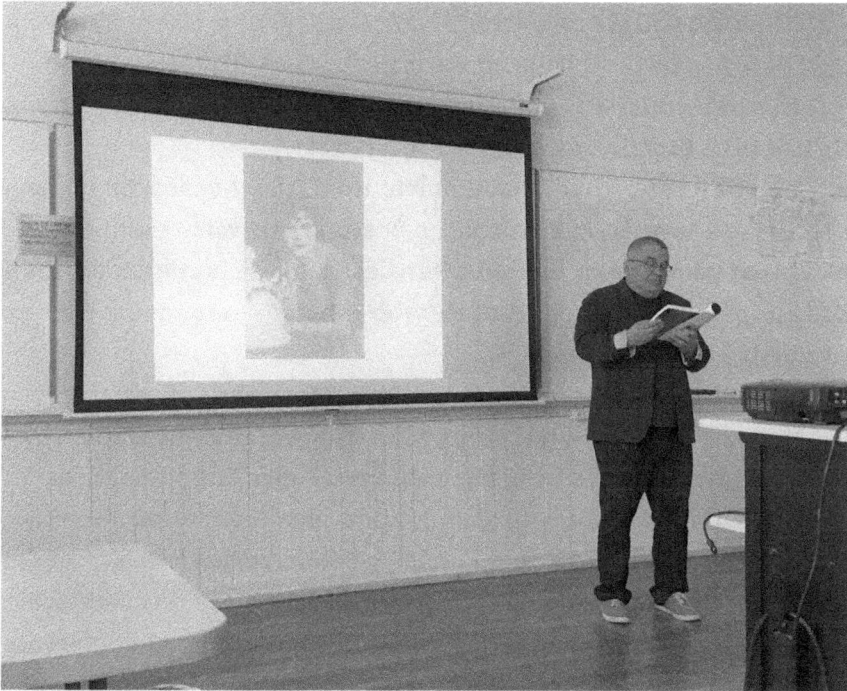

Microhistorian David Romo.

MARCH 17, 2023

The friend and colleague I usually ride with, is away, so I go to the cathedral on foot this time. I decide to drive and park a little closer to the bridge to shorten the walk. Even so, after being on my feet for hours, I am grateful that the El Paso streetcars are running in the afternoon so I can save a few steps.

My day serving at the cathedral in Juárez goes something like this:

"Where are you from?"

"Venezuela."

"How did you get to Juárez?"

"Part way on foot. Then on the train."

This individual was not telling me that he'd ridden inside a train. He had been literally riding on top of a boxcar.

Freight trains that come north from the Mexico/Guatemala border are known as *la Bestia* or the Beast. These trains are one of the ways that people with limited means get to these borderlands. It's a dangerous undertaking. People who hitch a ride on them are routinely killed or maimed.

Around 1,000 people attempted to cross to the U.S. on the Paso del Norte bridge last Sunday and were stopped. Evidently, there had been an internet post saying the border was open. Rumors spread.

The following day, 500 people rode into the city on la Bestia. Though the numbers of people released from authorities in El Paso lately have been averaging a manageable 200 per day, hundreds more are arriving in Ciudad Juárez every day. At a press conference on Monday, the mayor of Juárez said he would be cracking down. Cristina warns people to be careful and to stay away from the bridge.

On the days I've helped out at the cathedral, we've been serving around 400. Today, over 800 people show up. What we are able to offer would only fill the bellies of the children. I leave after we run out of food around 3 p.m.

Serving a meal at the cathedral.

MARCH 19, 2023

With the recent influx of guests from Haiti, I am inspired to do a little research on the history of the country. I learn that under French rule, Haiti was the most lucrative colony in the world. After the world's largest slave revolt in 1791, Haiti declared its independence in 1804. My jaw drops to learn that the price for that freedom was being forced to pay reparations to France. It took over one hundred years to pay off the debt, the equivalent of around twenty to thirty billion in today's dollars. Marlene Daut, University of Virginia Professor of African Diaspora Studies, called it "the greatest heist in history."[1]

The example of a country led by former slaves did not sit well with wealthy countries at a time when their economies were dependent on forced labor. The U.S. also sabotaged Haiti's development in a variety of ways, including its occupation of the country for almost twenty years in the early twentieth century and its control of Haiti's finances until 1947. That ensured a significant amount of its national income would be funneled to France and the U.S. for servicing its debt. Haiti could only pay the debt by cutting down and selling timber, denuding their hills and ruining their ecosystem. It doesn't appear to be an accident that Haiti is now the poorest country in the Western hemisphere.

After thousands of Haitian people were deported from the U.S. border in 2021, Special Envoy to Haiti Daniel Foote resigned, saying: "I will not be associated with the United States' inhumane, counterproductive decision to deport thousands of Haitian refugees..."[2] back to a country in desperate economic circumstances, where violent gangs control daily life. Most of the people who were deported had fled the country in 2010 to Latin America after a devastating earthquake. Many of the children deported had been born in another country and never lived in Haiti.

MARCH 22, 2023

As I write this, two Border Patrol vehicles are racing down the street in front of the house where I'm staying...

It's great to have my shift partner back. The mom of one of our long-term volunteers is with us for a few weeks. She brought a friend with her, and it looks like they're having great fun working together.

Danny makes his weekly visit to look in on our injured guests. As part of the same collaboration between Doctors of the World and Texas Tech, other guests are now able to see a doctor on Thursday evenings. The parents of an adorable three-year-old from Haiti who's been sick for over a week sign up right away. Dad writes us all a little love note in English on his cell phone, grateful for the warm welcome. Gangs are said to be in control of half of the country.

Three families recently left for Washington, D.C. I feel a little pang when I think of them. They have no friends or family there and are staying in shelters. This has become typical. It feels like a new phase. It's unsettling. We'll likely never hear if they were granted asylum.

One of our new guests has a wife and child who weren't allowed to cross with him into the U.S. I'm not sure why. He has all their papers and is wondering what to do. He ends up taking a taxi across the border and makes it back. This family plans to return home to Mexico, to one of the states that's also wracked by gang violence and organized crime.

Someone from Las Americas drops off an individual who has just been granted asylum. Authorities took him directly to the airport. But he had no ticket. Other complications prevented him from traveling on the spot. A kind observer gave him taxi fare to the legal folks. He'll stay with us for a few days, and Las Americas will help with travel arrangements.

Border Patrol stops by shortly after that with someone who came over the wall and will need surgery. At least she doesn't have one of those external fixators digging into her flesh. She is still in quite a bit of pain.

The guest who was hospitalized and treated for a serious infection around her external fixator is home after her operation. She and her daughter want to travel today. We're getting conflicting reports as to whether the airline will allow her to board, even with a bulkhead seat. She cannot bend her knee. They refused her once already early on in her stay, so we're concerned.

A colleague's new red bike.

A colleague proudly shows off a handsome new red bike. They had kept the old one in our small parking lot where it had been gradually dismembered. Finally, even the remains disappeared. This one will be kept inside.

MARCH 23, 2023

When I began to make a weekly trip to the cathedral in Juárez, we were serving a meal to around 400 people. On other days, they would serve as many as 600. A week ago, I was told, 1,000 people showed up.

After each group is seated, Cristina asks new arrivals to raise their hand. She speaks at some length. I feel the urgency her energy conveys. She explains that locals have been living with a river of humanity passing through their city for many years. She said they are tired of it. Would I be drained of compassion and concern for the situation if there were hundreds on the streets of downtown Petoskey or Cheboygan asking for money and sleeping at the entrances to the shops?

She asks people not to gather at the bridge, on the cathedral steps, or the pedestrian avenue. She reminds them of their vulnerability and asks them to be very careful, especially with people who ask for money in return for promises. She tells the new arrivals that there are attorneys and paralegals from several organizations at the cathedral from Monday to Thursday to offer legal support at no charge. Staff from the United Nations High Commissioner for Refugees are also on site to offer a variety of services, including transportation to shelters that are spread out all over the city.

As always, we serve many children accompanied by one or both parents. I remember one mom and her four kids. She looked particularly fatigued. All of the children asked for seconds. Mom said they were starving. My eyes continue to fill up regularly on my visits. What would a culture of care look like? It might look like the communities of care scattered across the borderlands, medicine in a dominant culture of violence, exploitation, and power over others.

Betty and I had agreed to meet at the cathedral. She likes to stop by a few times a week to talk with some of the people. After I finish up, we go to La Nueva Central for lunch. It's wonderful to take some time to rest, catch up, and have something to eat before walking back to El Paso. I leave feeling refreshed.

Volunteers are always encouraged to eat something at the cathedral during a break. But we're always running out of food, and I don't feel like eating until we've finished.

On the bridge, I'm learning to take time to stop, look around, and notice. At the top of the bridge, I see five people and a dog walking east on the U.S. side of the river with the border wall to their left.

Unless you're on one of the bridges, you can't even see the river. Every time I see it, my body registers the shock. Now a sluggish, nearly stagnant trail of liquid, the river looks more like a series of puddles in some places. People can easily wade across it from the Mexican side before they're confronted with the wall, razor wire, cameras, lights, jeeps, and people in uniform with weapons. I visited Big Bend National park for a few days last year. It was good to see the river with two names in that beautiful place, flowing wild and free.

IN CONTRAST to the streets of downtown Juárez, for the moment, downtown El Paso is back to the way it was before a state of emergency was declared last December and the convention center was turned into a shelter.

The situation may change again in May when the public health emergency for Covid-19 is lifted. The Title 42 Covid ban closed the border to over two million people seeking to enter the U.S. to claim asylum over the past three years. People see no alternative and come over the wall.

MARCH 29, 2023

Today the Vatican formally repudiated the Doctrine of Discovery, a series of papal bulls issued in the late fifteenth century. It was used as one of the earliest principles of international law for Christian monarchies to justify conquest and colonial rule by the nations of Europe.

The Doctrine of Discovery justified the violent appropriation of the lands European explorers "discovered," converting the original inhabitants to Christianity, along with their enslavement or extermination. Its impact was enormous: from the mid-1500s to the mid-2000s, most of the world beyond Europe became colonized under its legal cover. The Indigenous peoples of the Americas, who had long inhabited their ancestral lands, were dispossessed and became the victims of what Maria Yellow Horse Brave Heart and Lemyra M. DeBruyn call the American Indian Holocaust.[3]

The premise of the doctrine became part of U.S. jurisprudence. Thomas Jefferson, as Secretary of State, asserted that the Doctrine of Discovery should be applied to U.S. governance. The Supreme Court has cited it from 1823 to 2005.[4]

I appreciate Bill Ayers's summary of Roxanne Dunbar-Ortiz's *An Indigenous Peoples' History of the United States*. He says the author "strips us of our forged innocence, shocks us into new awarenesses, and draws a straight line from...settler-colonialism, the doctrine of discovery, the myth of manifest destiny, white supremacy, theft, and systematic killing—to the contemporary condition of permanent war, invasion and occupation, mass incarceration, and the constant use and threat of state violence. Best of all, she points a way beyond amnesia, paralyzing guilt, or helplessness toward discovering our deepest humanity in a project of truth-telling and repair."[5]

I share my limited but growing understanding of how we got here in that spirit. I am grateful to be learning from the witness and perspectives of people who have a different lived experience than the ones I was exposed to earlier in life.

MARCH 30, 2023

We are still digesting the shock, the circumstances, and the loss of life after the fire at a detention center in Ciudad Juárez on Monday. Looking back, Cristina's words to our guests last week were prophetic. Tensions have been building over the past few weeks. The mayor had promised to crack down. Reports said the crackdown began on the morning of the fire when people were being pulled off the street.

The Mexican government asserted almost immediately that the fire was started by the detainees. It's not clear how those being held could have started a fire when everything people are carrying is routinely taken away in detention. Even shoelaces are removed from shoes. A homicide investigation is underway. People were left locked in their cells as video appears to show security guards leaving the facility.

I am back in Juárez again. As usual, we have a few bags of clothing along with a few cases of cereal and other edibles with us. Our house coordinator from El Paso is here this time along with a few A-house volunteers. They are giving up their day off to lend a hand and show some solidarity. We knew the local team would be hurting. Some of the younger people who help serve know what our guests are going through because they've been there. The current situation brings back difficult memories.

There are hugs and lots of smiles as we greet each other and go about the work. It feels particularly comforting to be together again this week. I don't mind saying I cried before heading back to Mexico. I imagine many/most of us here have cried from time to time this week. It feels good to release some of the tensions and sorrow before they get stuck in the body.

After the first group is seated, forty candles on a central table are lit in silence, each one by a different person. Every flame honors someone who died in the fire. Images of the flags of the nations they came from are displayed on the backs of chairs. Many more are injured and in the hospital.

Forty candles are lit in silence to honor the forty people who perished in the fire at a detention center.

We serve around 700 people, including at least one mother and a daughter who had lost a partner and a father in the blaze—new trauma added to the trauma of the journey, the uncertainties, and what it takes to survive on the streets. People can seem like they're taking it all in stride as they gaze at their phones...

My friend is drawn into a conversation with a family of new arrivals as we were about to leave.

"Can you help us find shelter?"

"There are U.N. staff here who will drive your family to a shelter where there is space for you."

"Will we be safe there?"

The initial coverage of the fire claimed it had taken place in a shelter, not a detention center, which is basically a jail. No wonder Dad is concerned.

"Maybe we'll be safer on the street."

My friend mentions she caught part of a video someone was watching. Apparently, it's being circulated on social media. It promises that the U.S. is offering visas for people seeking asylum. The speaker appears to be an official. It's often difficult to be able to tell what is real. Things are often not as they appear to be in this hall of mirrors.

Serving a meal.

After leaving the cathedral, we drop off some supplies at the shelter where the food we serve on Thursdays is prepared. The stop lasts longer than anticipated. One of the people staying there had a lot of questions for my companion and needed some support. Staying in the car, my body relaxes into the quiet. I take the time to look into the clear blue skies and notice the lemony-limey shade of green that new leaves wear this time of year. How the tree nation pulls this off in the desert where it rains so seldom is a mystery. How people we support are as resilient as they are is another mystery.

There is almost no traffic and no wait as we cross the bridge. It's a first for me, sailing through like that. The border patrol agent is courteous this time, and we are grateful not to be peppered with questions.

APRIL 2023

APRIL 5, 2023

We are offered a break from furious spring winds that threaten wildfires and carry particles that clog the sinuses. My shift partner and I have little time to take a breath. One piece of good news: for the first time in my two winters at A-house, we have no injured guests staying with us.

I arrive for duty in the early morning hours. I track the movement of the seasons by the presence or absence of light in the sky. The volunteer on the overnight shift briefs me on a situation with a family from Venezuela. Mom and her daughter arrived, as expected, yesterday. Mom was eagerly awaiting news of her husband and other daughter, hospitalized with an asthma attack. Volunteers had been trying unsuccessfully to reach the hospital. When I call after breakfast, I am told the girl was discharged yesterday. Where did they go?

Mom has no phone, but she does have her husband's phone number, a Mexican number. Dan sends Dad a text via WhatsApp, asking him to call the house. It doesn't take long to get a response. Dad and daughter spent the night at a shelter I've never visited. The walk from there to here would only take about twenty minutes, but something tells me to get in the car and pick them up. Mom and daughter go with me.

The little shelter looks like a daycare center with an abundance of young children. It used to give people who work in the fields a place to rest. Everyone sleeps on the floor, keeping warm with Red Cross blankets. The volunteer staff are friendly and offer to host the entire family, but we can offer them their own room with bunk beds. (Our single guests and couples without children sleep in dorms). Dad collects his things from the floor, and we leave. As we drive back to A-house, Dad looks around the streets thoughtfully.

"We were out here last night, wandering around lost for hours until after midnight, looking for a place to stay. It was cold. Our daughter was just getting over an asthma attack, and she was coughing and crying."

He says his daughter was discharged around 8 p.m. They left with no guidance from the hospital.

Authorities had made us aware of the family's situation before anyone arrived. It seems like the hospital would have known too. This wasn't the hospital we usually deal with and may not be as experienced with the needs of people like these.

This is a family who fled cartel violence in their home country. These cartels with their threats and extortion are vicious.

In the early afternoon, we welcome a family of six, including a child with autism and epilepsy who was also released after a brief hospital stay. I want to take a photo of the enormous, handsome new bus they arrive in, but it's gone before I can act. Dad comes from one Central American country. Mom is from another. The kids were all born in Mexico. Unsettled lives. Soon after we finish lunch and cleanup, another family arrives.

I sit with them at one of the tables in the common room to get them registered. Knowing we are expecting fifteen additional guests, a colleague offers to set out the many sets of sheets and towels everyone will need.

"Are you hungry?" I ask the parents.

Yes. Dad grimaces and says he is having digestive problems and is in quite a bit of pain. Without hesitation, the guests who prepared lunch offer to make a hot soup. Another guest offers to take sheets and towels up to their room. After the simple meal, they will be able to take a shower and rest. Dad feeds the child with special needs.

The other guests we are expecting are dropped off at shift change.

Everyone pulls together. With that comes a feeling of grace that is palpable and carries us through our days.

APRIL 13, 2023

I work my last shift at A-house and make my last journey to Ciudad Juárez today. I will be folding up my tent in less than a week and heading for home.

There was an exciting change in the meal service: a new supply of reusable plates and glasses! This will both create more work and significantly reduce the waste generated from all the styrofoam cups and plates—not to mention the cost savings. Two of the young volunteers had their hands full with the dishwashing detail.

There is endless strangeness here in the borderlands, and the sands are ever shifting. Instead of serving a growing number of people—from 700 to 1,000 lately—only a few hundred showed up on Thursday.

Rumors and videos of someone who appears to be an authority continue. Gate 36 in the border wall was apparently open for a time as the figure in the video promised. People were allowed to walk through and were loaded onto unmarked white buses. We saw one of these buses in town, full of people, pulling out yesterday morning.

There are many tactics to create the appearance that these political borders are secure and everything is under control. No expense is too much. Powerful forces are sweeping through the world.

APRIL 17, 2023

Whose land? Today, El Paso lies within the political borders of the U.S. Before that it was part of Mexico. And before that the territory of various tribal peoples.

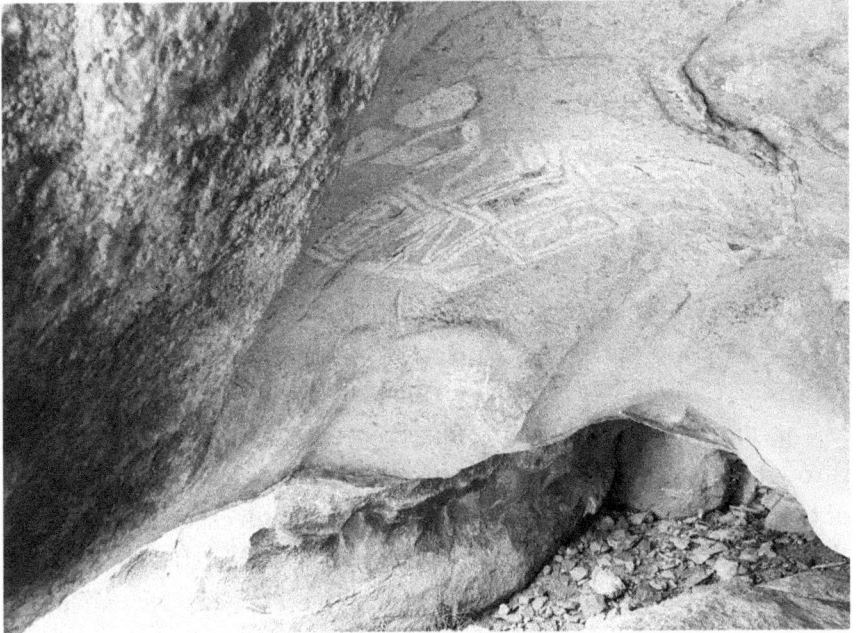

Ancient pictographs at Hueco Tanks State Park.

A friend and I take a guided walk to see some of the ancient pictographs at Hueco Tanks, a state park named for its natural rock basins. The igneous rock formations are on unceded lands (Indigenous lands that were never signed over to the United States) sacred to the Mescalero Apache, Kiowa, Comanche, and other tribal peoples.

Our young guide begins by reminding us that it is a privilege for all of us to be able to enjoy the park. Back in the day, young people came there to party. Others came to picnic and hike. A developer wanted to turn it into a resort. One of the photos shows an unnaturally even place between the rock formations, the site of a dam intended to create a lake in the desert. It didn't work. Our guide encourages us to take the time to learn something about the history and cultures of the places we visit.

Claret Cup Cactus.

Whose land? Some are suggesting these parks be returned to the care and experience of native peoples. Several co-stewardship agreements have recently been signed in various parks, like Utah's Bears Ears National Monument and Michigan's Sanilac Petroglyphs State Historical Park. Putting these different ways of knowing together in relationship with one another seems very promising and respectful of the wisdom and practices of Indigenous peoples.

Our guide mentions that trash such as glass and aluminum cans older than fifty years are also preserved as history. The Claret Cup Cactus is in bloom and abundant.

APRIL 20, 2023

On my last full day in El Paso, I tag along with a small BAE group to a talk by Carlos Marentes. I have been looking forward to meeting this Facebook friend I've heard so much about for the first time.

Carlos is the founder and director of *Sin Fronteras* or the Border Agricultural Workers Project. The project opened the center we visited near the Paso del Norte port of entry in 1994. It has provided a safe place for these hardworking people to rest, have a meal, and build relationships and solidarity. That center now offers shelter to increasing numbers of people migrating north.

A meeting of Sin Fronteras *or Border Agricultural Workers Project.*

Carlos is a long-time advocate for the dignity and well-being of agricultural workers, people mostly from the north of Mexico who labor long hours in the fields in oppressive conditions to put food on our tables. Carlos invites us to shift from taking the food we buy for granted and instead see food as something sacred and worthy of deep respect.

After we arrive at the center, we walk through the room I described a few weeks ago when I came to pick up the "lost" husband and daughter of an A-house guest. This time, I say hello to a group of young people just before we head upstairs to the meeting room.

"Spanish?" I ask.

"English!" they announce.

It is the first Afghani family I've met here in El Paso.

The talk is moving and informative. I imagine these laborers bedding down for the night at the center. But Carlos says it's not like that. People looking for work must show up near the bridge around midnight. Those chosen for the day might arrive in the fields at 2 a.m. or 3 a.m. Their work begins in the darkness.

Plastic discs are passed around the group. People earn one for filling a large container, like the one in the background, to the brim with chili peppers, onions, or other produce. Later, you turn in the discs for cash, each being worth around sixty-five to seventy cents. After your workday ends, you get just a few hours of rest and a meal before heading out again into the night. The workers who come from Mexico are away from home and their families, on average, for eight months a year.

Carlos said something that continues to haunt me: "We used to be able to take care of ourselves." Interdependence is the reality of life as I understand it. Dependency is something very different. It leaves us vulnerable to control and harm.

A LAST REFLECTION

INTEGRATING THE EXPERIENCE

It's been five years since I was first drawn to the borderlands. I wanted to see for myself what goes on here, to learn about the circumstances, both individual and collective, that compel people to leave their homeland, culture, language, and often, their families behind.

I came back the second time because I missed the community—and the sweetness and the demands of the work. The needs include not only food, shelter, clothing, and sanitation, but also mutual respect, belonging, and emotional and spiritual support. Over these years, my Spanish has improved to the point where I am finally able to have the conversations I wanted to have on my first visit. I still make lots of grammatical mistakes, but no one seems to mind. I also get to use my French. I am enjoying learning a little Haitian Kreyòl and am enchanted by its musicality.

As a community volunteer during my third winter in El Paso, I began to connect many dots—geographic, historic, the echoes of trauma across generations. A bigger picture richer with common themes, complexities, nuances, and contradictions began to emerge.

I also had the chance to get a taste of what life is like in Ciudad Juárez. The violence done to Mexican culture feels impossibly heavy.

The desert is a foreign land for someone who has spent a lifetime around water. I've learned to appreciate its simple, austere beauty and how tough and resilient life must be to survive. As the planet continues to scorch, summers are becoming unbearably hot. I wonder if we will see nation states falling away. These structures have only existed for a few hundred years. They are not how people have addressed their greatest challenges over time. An unprecedented level of global cooperation and solidarity will be needed in the years ahead in the interests of life and our very survival.

I continue to refer to the people we serve as people and chafe against labels like "migrants," or worse, "aliens." Labels can be useful to describe situations and make distinctions. Applied to people, labels separate us from one another. Divide and conquer is a tried-and-true military principle. In these times of growing polarization, it is becoming easier to see how it is being leveraged and wielded as a tool of domination and control.

Maybe one of the most important shifts we could make is to see ourselves as part of one human family embedded in a greater circle of life. We come from different circumstances with different histories, but we share a common humanity. Our guests are people who make choices they feel are in their best interests. We all do.

What I want for others is what I want for myself: to be able to safely remain at home with my family, friends, community, language, and culture; to be able to support myself; to have the opportunity to grow in my humanity; to express my creativity together with others; to move freely in the world; and to engage in this larger adventure called life. For that to be possible, the governments of wealthy countries like ours would need to inflict less damage on the world.

The significant harm done by the United States government, and those of other wealthy countries, fuels migration—leading people to leave their homes, communities, language, culture, and ancestral lands. This takes a toll on culture, tradition, and ancestral knowledge and connection. The industrialized world is said to be spending over twice as much, on average, on arming their borders as on climate mitigation and adaptation. It's not clear what will be asked of us in the years ahead.

Population growth and climate destabilization will be additional global drivers of involuntary migration going forward. The number of people who will be on the move is mind-boggling. According to the Institute for Economics and Peace, 1.2 billion people could be displaced from their homes by 2050.[1] The displaced will not only include people from faraway lands and islands, but also millions of people from coastal cities like Miami. Sea levels will continue to rise as land ice continues to melt. Floods and hurricanes will continue to grow more intense and frequent. People will continue to flee the wildfires that are growing more intense and more frequent—with a longer fire season.

Laws have not kept up with these realities. You could be living in a region where suffocating heat and natural disasters from climate instability no longer allow food to be grown. Your island nation could be slowly going under the waves. Those affected by these situations are not legally recognized as refugees today, and they are not entitled to asylum protections.

When it comes to the big issues around immigration, I am convinced that laws and policies can never substitute for a healthy culture and the bonds of relationship in community. I am learning that culture is something much deeper and essential to the health of a people than I had ever imagined. It is more than the aesthetics of architecture, language, music, dance, cooking, and more. It is what connects us with Earth and the cosmos. It is what teaches us that we have responsibilities to one another and to life. I experience modern culture as ungrounded, morally adrift.

I've come to understand that there is a greater law of life that compels us to make some effort to relieve the suffering of the stranger in our midst. For laws to be considered just, they must be in alignment with the larger realities and ecosystems in which we dwell. Only then can they act as a force for healing and repair. That view is also reflected in the thought of Flavia Valguisti, Director of the Institute of Neuroscience and Law and former judge of child and family cases in Argentina. Valguisti sees the potential for justice systems to be a force for healing and transformative when aligned with what she calls the Law of Life. These are universal principles that are life-giving and life-affirming.[2] What we know as modern culture is ungrounded in these principles. Maybe that's the source of so much of the growing violence in our world.

I continue to remember my own ancestors from Europe who left everything behind. I wonder what things were like for them both on the journey and as they became settlers participating in a large colonial enterprise. They crossed the Atlantic for many of the same reasons people continue to leave the world they know behind: war, poverty, famine, religious intolerance, violence, loss of land, a longing for a "better" life. On my first journey to Europe, I felt something I could not put into words at the time. While I have a love for northern Michigan as the place I call home, I feel disconnected from my ancestral lands and feel the emptiness one feels without a rich cultural life.

I reflect on the ongoing impact of mass migration from Europe on the original peoples of this land and the reclaiming of culture. I remember the Middle Passage and the people from Africa who were trafficked here for their enslavement. I think about the ongoing history of separating children from their families.

The history and toll over generations of forced displacement is something I continue to find sobering. During my last winter in El Paso, I came across several articles and a documentary called *A Long Journey: The Hidden Jews of the Southwest* by accident. What I learned astounded me. The assertion, based on genetic research, is that up to 25% of the entire Hispanic population of the United States has Jewish DNA.[3] How could this be?

It goes back to the Spanish Inquisition in the fifteenth century when, literally, the day after Christopher Columbus sailed for the West Indies, Jewish people who refused to convert to Christianity were expelled from Spain. One of the conversos, or crypto-Jews, who converted or pretended to convert became close to the monarchy and was granted land in Nueva Leon, Mexico. Many *conversos* fled there for safety. Later, the conquistador and explorer from New Spain, Don Juan de Oñate, led some of these people from Zacatecas to Nuevo México, then part of New Spain.

I was aware that forced displacement has been a historical reality for the Jewish people. Now I learned that displacement is a theme found all around the world. Its accompanying collective trauma, often hidden, can take generations to come back to consciousness for healing and repair. Unhealed trauma repeats itself over and over again.

I am very moved by the examples of these *converso* families reclaiming this aspect of their family history in a variety of ways. I am saddened by the different wounds so many of us carry from our unique family and collective histories. Multiply this by the histories and people who cross borders all over the world. I am also inspired by the reclaiming of culture and story I see among Indigenous peoples across North America and beyond. Has humanity reached a point in our evolution where we can see one another as members of one human family in a greater circle of life?

As I write these last thoughts, Gaza is being devastated with unconditional military and political support for Israel by the United States government. But we have the invitation to develop more skillful means to transform conflict in creative and generative ways. We need economic systems that are aligned with life, rather than preying upon it. War is designed to devastate. It devastates not only human beings in body and soul, communities, and culture, but also the sacred sources of life we all depend on for our very survival: clean water and air, healthy soil, energy, and a climate stable enough to grow food. Given accelerating global scorching, any war now needs to be considered a war against life itself. We could also see that the land does not belong to us. It is we who belong to the land. We are invited to learn to commit to an ethic of life. Everything we've ever loved is at stake.

El Paso is a gentle city with a culture of relationship. At the same time, militarized borders keep the local economy humming. Immigration and Customs Enforcement, Customs and Border Protection, the Federal Bureau of Investigation, Fort Bliss, the border wall, checkpoints, helicopters, dogs, weaponry, surveillance, detention centers, courts, care for unaccompanied young people and the medical care our guests receive after breaking their bodies scaling the border wall is costing so much. Perhaps the material cost is the least of it.

The nearly 2,000-mile border between Mexico and the United States is said to be the most frequently crossed border in the world and the most dangerous land crossing, according to the United Nations.[4] It is the nature of life to move and flow. Political borders interfere with natural processes and attempt to control them by force. This requires a level of violence, repression, and expense that is chilling.

The sight of the river with two names, barely flowing, held in place with a straitjacket of cement, its life-giving waters bled away, feels wrong. It's not difficult to sense the fear and defensiveness that lie behind the will to interfere with and wield control over natural processes. Pressures are building on the barriers that are preventing life from flowing and moving freely. Eventually, the dams we've built will have to give way.

As many now observe, we are living through the end of a major chapter of history. Powerful winds of transformation are sweeping through our world. It is a time of reckoning and grieving where much is beyond our ability to control. Sharing our losses and joy together in community is essential medicine that will facilitate this collective transformation. Traditional cultures understood that sharing sorrow helps us clip the cords of loyalty to the status quo and create space for what is to come. It also helps ground some of the historical pain and collective trauma of the world in our shared body where it can be digested and metabolized—and eventually transformed and healed.

Modern life can feel like a bubble, a series of somewhat safe and predictable experiences carefully crafted that have shielded me from a rawer experience of living. The strange thing is, if you lived in many places in El Paso, even a mile from the border, Sacred Heart Church, the bus stations, and the shelters, you would have little idea of what is going on. It is the same for most of us who live comfortable lives, apart from the experience of the ones who bear the brunt of them. By opening my eyes and my heart, this humble work of hospitality and solidarity has been medicine. I feel forever changed by the experience, a little softer, maybe a little humbler. I do not wish to be protected from the cries of the children, nor do I wish to be overtaken by the darkness. The world, mercifully, does not depend on me for salvation.

Could this larger community of care I've experienced and been part of over these past years be a model to heal and repair our relationships with one another and the larger circle of being? Could it be an antidote to the violence that is plaguing societies at every level? Mutual aid happens spontaneously in cities and rural areas around the world over time. The emerging movement to heal collective trauma is growing stronger, even as violence and ill will inflict massive amounts of trauma in the world. Those groups and nations that have experienced colonial oppression are rising up with moral courage and moral authority. My prayer is that we become more skillful and committed to the challenging and often painful work of healing and repairing our relationships with each other. The structure of the old order is ill-equipped for the future and is crumbling around us. A period of chaos and not knowing is a phase of transition to be anticipated. For me, a deep and unshakable trust in the seasons and cycles of life is what having faith means.

As I pack my bags and prepare to return home, I'll go up to Scenic Drive one last time as the full moon rises and the sun sets. The lights of the sister cities will begin to twinkle. From there, it all looks like one big city, cradled by the mountains with a river, cemented in, and lined with flood lights, moving slowly, on its own journey to join the open waters.

It is spring, and the winged ones high in the air are returning to their summer home in the north country.

NOTES

MAP OF THE SISTER CITIES

1. "Vector Map of the Texan El Paso County, United States," Shutterstock, Accessed February 6, 2024, https://www.shutterstock.com/image-vector/vector-map-texan-el-paso-county-1903913389.

MAP OF BORDERS WHEN MOST OF THE U.S. SOUTHWEST WAS PART OF MEXICO

1. E.W.A. Rowles, *United States at Beginning of Mexican War 1846*, map, *Library of Congress* (Modern School Supply Co.), https://www.loc.gov/resource/g3701sm.gct00483/?sp=25&r=0.088,0.459,0.44,0.224,0.

MAP OF EARLY INDIAN TRIBES

1. "National Atlas. Indian Tribes, Cultures & Languages: [United States]," Library of Congress, Geography and Map Division, Accessed February 6, 2024, https://www.loc.gov/resource/g3701e.ct003648r/?r=0.873,0.247,0.124,0.078,0.

NOVEMBER 2019

1. "Migrant Protection Protocols," U.S. Department of Homeland Security, January 24, 2019, https://www.dhs.gov/news/2019/01/24/migrant-protection-protocols#:~:text=The%20Migrant%20Protection%20Protocols%20(MPP,of%20their%20immigration%20proceedings%2C%20where.
2. "Central American Migration: Root Causes and U.S. Policy," Congressional Research Service, March 27, 2019, https://sgp.fas.org/crs/row/IF11151.pdf.

DECEMBER 2019

1. Jim Parker, "On anniversary of immigrant surge, head of El Paso's Annunciation House looks back on whirlwind year," ABC-7, December 2, 2019, https://kvia.com/news/border/2019/12/02/on-anniversary-of-immigrant-surge-head-of-el-pasos-annunciation-house-looks-back-on-whirlwind-year/.
2. "Wolverine Worldwide PFAS Statement," Plainfield Charter Township, accessed

January 25, 2024, https://www.plainfieldmi.org/information_about/pfas_settle
ment/index.php.

3. Todd Miller, *Storming the Wall: Climate Change, Migration, and Homeland Security* (San Francisco: City Lights Books, 2017), 24.

4. "Cumulative carbon dioxide (CO_2) emissions from fossil fuel combustion world-wide from 1750 to 2022, by major country," Statistica, Accessed February 6, 2024, https://www.statista.com/statistics/1007454/cumulative-co2-emissions-world wide-by-country/.

5. "United States Imports By Country," Trading Economics, Accessed February 6, 2024, https://tradingeconomics.com/united-states/imports-by-country.

6. Ousmane Diagana, "3 key fronts on which Africa must combat climate change," World Bank Blogs, October 28, 2022. https://blogs.worldbank.org/africacan/3-key-fronts-which-africa-must-combat-climate-change.

7. "Fort Bliss Army Base Guide," Military.com, accessed January 25, 2024, https://www.military.com/base-guide/fort-bliss.

JANUARY 2020

1. Sam Biddle, "Amazon Co-Owns Deportation Airline Implicated in Alleged Torture of Immigrants," *The Intercept*, February 17, 2022, https://theintercept.com/2022/02/17/amazon-ice-deportation-flights-omni/.

2. "Credible Fear Screenings," U.S. Citizenship and Immigration Services, August 7, 2023, https://www.uscis.gov/humanitarian/refugees-and-asylum/asylum/credi ble-fear-screenings.

FEBRUARY 2020

1. *Harvest of Empire: The Untold Story of Latinos in America,* directed by Peter Getzels and Eduardo Lopez (Getzels Gordon Productions, 2012).

2. "Report: Forced to Flee Central America's Northern Triangle," Doctors Without Borders, May 11, 2017, https://www.doctorswithoutborders.org/latest/report-forced-flee-central-americas-northern-triangle.

3. "After the Coup," Human Rights Watch, December 20, 2010, https://www.hrw.org/report/2010/12/20/after-coup/ongoing-violence-intimidation-and-impunity-honduras.

MARCH 2020

1. Alan Sandstrom,"The Virgin Guadalupe and Tonantzin," Mexicolore, January 30, 2011, https://www.mexicolore.co.uk/aztecs/gods/virgin-of-guadalupe-and-tonantzin.

2. "42 U.S.C," Gov Info, accessed January 27, 2024, https://www.govinfo.gov/content/pkg/USCODE-2011-title42/html/USCODE-2011-title42-chap6A-subchapII-partG.

htm#:~:text=The%20Surgeon%20General%2C%20with%20the,or%20posses
sion%20into%20any%20other.

REBIRTH

1. From "Complaint of El Rio Grande" by Richard Blanco, *How to Love a Country: Poems* by Richard Blanco, Copyright © 2019 by Richard Blanco, Reprinted by permission of Beacon Press, Boston.
2. "Facts and figures: Regularization and protection of Venezuelan nationals in Colombia, Ecuador, Peru and Chile," Amnesty International, September 21, 2023, https://www.amnesty.org/en/latest/news/2023/09/facts-figures-venezuelans-colombia-ecuador-peru-chile/#:~:text=1%20in%204%20people%20in,%2C%20and%20Chile%20(444%2C000.

JANUARY 2023

1. James Barragán,"Without evidence, Gov. Greg Abbott asks whether nonprofits are helping migrants enter Texas," *Texas Tribune*, December 15, 2022, https://www.texastribune.org/2022/12/15/greg-abbott-texas-migrants-border-nonprofits/.
2. "Central American Migration: Root Causes and U.S. Policy," Congressional Research Service, March 27, 2019, https://sgp.fas.org/crs/row/IF11151.pdf.

FEBRUARY 2023

1. https://centrodesantacatalina.org/products/

MARCH 2023

1. Marlene Daut, "When France Extorted Haiti—The Greatest Heist in History," *The Conversation*, June 30, 2020, https://theconversation.com/when-france-extorted-haiti-the-greatest-heist-in-history-137949.
2. Anne Gearan, et al., "U.S. special envoy to Haiti resigns, says he will not be associated with 'inhumane, counterproductive' deportations of Haitians," *The Washington Post*, September 23, 2021, https://www.washingtonpost.com/politics/haiti-biden-deportations-envoy/2021/09/23/c8304424-1c6c-11ec-8380-5fbadbc43ef8_story.html.
3. Maria Yellow Horse Brave Heart, Ph.D., and Lemyra M. DeBruyn, Ph.D., "The American Indian Holocaust: Healing Historical Unresolved Grief," *American Indian and Alaska Native Mental Health Research* 8, no. 2 (1998): 60-82. https://doi.org/10.5820/aian.0802.1998.60.
4. Joshua Mark, "Doctrine of Discovery," *World History Encyclopedia*, October 11, 2023, https://www.worldhistory.org/Doctrine_of_Discovery/.
5. Bill Ayers, "Roxanne Dunbar-Ortiz, *An Indigenous Peoples' History of the United*

States," Bill Ayers, September 15, 2014, https://billayers.org/2014/09/15/roxanne-dunbar-ortiz-an-indigenous-peoples-history-of-the-united-states/.

INTEGRATING THE EXPERIENCE

1. Jon Henley, "Climate crisis could displace 1.2bn people by 2050, report warns," *The Guardian*, September 9, 2020, https://www.theguardian.com/environment/2020/sep/09/climate-crisis-could-displace-12bn-people-by-2050-report-warns.

2. Flavia Valgiusti, "Justice as Harmony," Youtube, September 26, 2023, https://www.youtube.com/watch?v=QnuTe6n6uv4.

3. *A Long Journey: The Hidden Jews of the Southwest*, directed by Isaac Artenstein (Cinewest, 2020).

4. "US-Mexico border, 'world's deadliest' overland migration route: IOM," United Nations, September 12, 2023, https://news.un.org/en/story/2023/09/1140622.

BIBLIOGRAPHY

Amnesty International. "Facts and figures: Regularization and protection of Venezuelan nationals in Colombia, Ecuador, Peru and Chile." September 21, 2023. https://www.amnesty.org/en/latest/news/2023/09/facts-figures-venezuelans-colombia-ecuador-peru-chile/

Ayers, Bill. "Roxanne Dunbar-Ortiz, *An Indigenous Peoples' History of the United States*." Bill Ayers. September 15, 2014. https://billayers.org/2014/09/15/roxanne-dunbar-ortiz-an-indigenous-peoples-history-of-the-united-states/.

Barragán, James. "Without evidence, Gov. Greg Abbott asks whether nonprofits are helping migrants enter Texas." *Texas Tribune*, December 15, 2022. https://www.texastribune.org/2022/12/15/greg-abbott-texas-migrants-border-nonprofits/.

Biddle, Sam. "Amazon Co-Owns Deportation Airline Implicated in Alleged Torture of Immigrants." *The Intercept*, February 17, 2022. https://theintercept.com/2022/02/17/amazon-ice-deportation-flights-omni/.

Brave Heart, Ph.D., Maria Yellow Horse and DeBruyn, Ph.D., Lemyra M. "The American Indian Holocaust: Healing Historical Unresolved Grief." *American Indian and Alaska Native Mental Health Research* 8, no. 2 (1998): 60-82. https://doi.org/10.5820/aian.0802.1998.60.

Cinewest (Producer) & Isaac Artenstein (Director). 2020. *A Long Journey: The Hidden Jews of the Southwest.*

Congressional Research Service. "Central American Migration: Root Causes and U.S. Policy." March 27, 2019. https://sgp.fas.org/crs/row/IF11151.pdf.

"Cumulative carbon dioxide (CO_2) emissions from fossil fuel combustion worldwide from 1750 to 2022, by major country." *Statistica*. Accessed February 6, 2024. https://www.statista.com/statistics/1007454/cumulative-co2-emissions-worldwide-by-country/.

Daut, Marlene. "When France extorted Haiti – the greatest heist in history." *The Conversation*. June 30, 2020. https://theconversation.com/when-france-extorted-haiti-the-greatest-heist-in-history-137949.

Diagana, Ousmane. "3 key fronts on which Africa must combat climate change." World Bank Blogs. October 28, 2022. https://blogs.worldbank.org/african/3-key-fronts-which-africa-must-combat-climate-change.

Doctors Without Borders. "Report: Forced to Flee Central America's Northern Triangle." May 11, 2017. https://www.doctorswithoutborders.org/latest/report-forced-flee-central-america's-northern-triangle.

Gearan, Anne, Hudson, John, Miroff, Nick, and Sullivan, Sean. "U.S. special envoy to Haiti resigns, says he will not be associated with 'inhumane, counterproductive deportations of Haitians." *The Washington Post.* September 23, 2021. https://theconversation.com/when-france-extorted-haiti-the-greatest-heist-in-history-137949.

Getzels Gordon Productions (Producer) & Peter Getzels and Eduardo Lopez, (Directors). (2012) *Harvest of Empire: The Untold Story of Latinos in America.*, 1 hr, 30 min. GovInfo. "42 U.S.C." Accessed January 27, 2024. https://tinyurl.com/y9xkaes8

Henley, Jon. "Climate crisis could displace 1.2bn people by 2050, report warns." *The Guardian.* September 9, 2020. https://www.theguardian.com/environment/2020/sep/09/climate-crisis-could-displace-12bn-people-by-2050-report-warns.

Humans Rights Watch. "After the Coup." December 20, 2010. https://www.hrw.org/report/2010/12/20/after-coup/ongoing-violence-intimidation-and-impunity-honduras.

Mark, Joshua. "Doctrine of Discovery." World History Encyclopedia. October 11, 2023. https://www.worldhistory.org/Doctrine_of_Discovery/.

Military.com. "Fort Base Army Base Guide." Accessed January 25, 2024. https://www.military.com/base-guide/fort-bliss.

Miller, Todd. *Storming the Wall: Climate Change, Migration, and Homeland Security.* San Francisco: City Lights Books, 2017.

"National Atlas. Indian Tribes, Cultures & Languages: [United States]." Library of Congress, Geography and Map Division. Accessed February 6, 2024. https://www.loc.gov/resource/g3701e.ct003648r/?r=0.873,0.247,0.124,0.078,0.

Parker, Jim. "On anniversary of immigrant surge, head of El Paso's Annunciation House looks back on whirlwind year." ABC-7. December 2, 2019. https://www.loc.gov/resource/g3701e.ct003648r/?r=0.873,0.247,0.124,0.078,0..

Plainfield Charter Township. "Wolverine Worldwide PFAS Statement." Accessed January 25, 2024. https://www.plainfieldmi.org/information_about/pfas_settle ment/index.php.

Sandstrom, Alan. "The Virgin Guadalupe and Tonantzin." *Mexicolore*, January 30, 2011. https://www.loc.gov/resource/g3701e.ct003648r/?r=0.873,0.247,0.124,0.078,0..

United Nations. "US-Mexico border, 'world's deadliest' overland migration route: IOM." September 12, 2023. https://news.un.org/en/story/2023/09/1140622.

"United States Digital Map Library." USGenWeb Archives. Accessed February 6, 2024. http://usgwarchives.net/maps/maps.html.

"United States Imports By Country." Trading Economics. Accessed February 6, 2024. https://tradingeconomics.com/united-states/imports-by-country.

U.S. Citizenship and Immigration Services. "Credible Fear Screenings." August 7, 2023. https://www.uscis.gov/humanitarian/refugees-and-asylum/asylum/credible-fear-screenings.

U.S. Department of Homeland Security. "Migrant Protection Protocols." January 24, 2019. https://www.dhs.gov/news/2019/01/24/migrant-protection-protocols#:~: text=The%20Migrant%20Protection%20Protocols%20(MPP,of%20their%20immi gration%20proceedings%2C%20where.

Valgiusti, Flavia. "Justice as Harmony." Youtube. September 26, 2023. https://www. youtube.com/watch?v=QnuTe6n6uv4.

"Vector Map of the Texan El Paso County, United States," Shutterstock, Accessed February 6, 2024, https://www.shutterstock.com/image-vector/vector-map-texan-el-paso-county-1903913389.

About the Author

DEB HANSEN has been a border-crosser and aspiring bridge-builder for a very long time: harvesting wisdom from cultures, languages, wisdom traditions, friendships, and livelihoods. Her life has been a labyrinth of twists and turns, purposeful only in hindsight. She taught French in higher education and worked creatively with IBM in marketing and communications. She could never have anticipated Interfaith ordination and service as a chaplain at a trauma hospital in Detroit later in life.

As a student of transformation, she has worked with individuals going through challenging times as a life and leadership coach and spiritual companion. Now she is also a student of collective transformation in communities and cultures reorienting to tradition, relationship, responsibility, reverence, respect, and care. Her work at the U.S./Mexico border and beyond is in the spirit of solidarity. She writes and speaks about her experience working in the borderlands and on behalf of the waters and climate of Michigan. She sees these times not only in terms of dangers, but also as a portal to fresh and life-giving possibilities. She intends her border-crossings to be a thread in a collective effort to weave a fragmented view of the world back together in ways that ground, heal, and bring joy and unity in diversity.

Moving beyond looking at issues in isolation, her work is about connecting dots and seeing patterns that bring greater depth and insight. She is drawn to beauty, poetry, the emerging movement to heal collective trauma, and an unfolding cultural transformation that is regrounding us.